THE RING OF THE NIBELUNG

THE RING OF THE NIBELUNG

BY

RICHARD WAGNER

Translated, and with a foreword, by STEWART ROBB
Introduction by EDWARD DOWNES

A Dutton  *Paperback*

Illustrations by JIM McMULLAN

NEW YORK
E. P. DUTTON

Library of Congress Card Catalog Number: 60-9686.

Dedicated to my son, Christopher

Contents

Introduction

It is no accident that Wagner's first written version of *The Ring* story, *The Nibelungen Myth as a Project for a Drama,* dates from 1848, the year of the Communist Manifesto.

Revolution was spreading like a prairie fire across Europe. The first smoldering spark had appeared in Sicily, but it was, as usual, Paris that gave the flaming signal: monarchs cowered and chancelleries trembled as the news of the February Revolution swept across the continent, raising barricades in the streets of peaceful cities, democratic hopes in the hearts of men, and fiery speeches from demagogues and dreamers.

As the wave reaches Dresden early in 1849 we even see the conductor of the Royal Opera, caught up in the general liberal excitement, haranguing a crowd of three thousand honest Dresdeners, members of a mildly republican *Vaterlandsverein.* His whole soul goes into a passionate appeal to the King of Saxony to shed the bonds of custom and caste and take true kingship upon himself by coming to the assistance of his impoverished and exploited working classes. He adjures the court aristocracy to renounce "the last remnant" of special privilege and hints at dire consequences if they refuse.

With a nervous eloquence for which he later became famous, this short, bespectacled gentleman with the large head and sensitive, intellectual profile explains to his amazed audience his dream of a socialistic society in which the ills caused by the pursuit of gold shall vanish.

"The question of the source of all misery of our present social condition must be the focus of our most steadfast and active attention," he declares. "We must make up our minds whether we really believe God can have doomed mankind, this crown of creation, with all its high spiritual and artistic capacities, to be held in abject slavery to a hard, unyielding product of nature, this sallow metal."

"The success I had was simply appalling," wrote Wagner. "The astounded audience seemed to remember nothing of the speech of the Royal Conductor save the incidental attack I had made on the court sycophants. The news of this incredible event spread like wildfire." His speech was published in full in the next day's issue of the Dresden *Anzeiger*.

When pandemonium finally broke loose in Dresden, Wagner did cast his lot with the poor and exploited against the rich and powerful. In later years, when he had found a protector in King Ludwig II of Bavaria, and he was dictating his autobiography to Cosima, he tended to minimize his record as a practical revolutionary. But there is considerable evidence that he was involved in the ordering and distribution of grenades and that he was regarded by his fellows on the Dresden barricades as a person of authority in the insurrectionary organization.

A warrant was issued for the arrest of the Royal Conductor, and he narrowly escaped imprisonment by fleeing to Switzerland. Several of his friends who had taken part in the Revolution, including August Röckel and Michael Bakunin, did receive death sentences, commuted to long prison terms.

Wagner, of course, lost his excellent position at the Dresden Opera and, for the moment at least, was ruined professionally, pecuniarily, and socially. Not until 1860 did he receive permission to set foot in German territory again, and it was another two years before he was granted amnesty in the kingdom of Saxony.

One of the first fruits of Wagner's exile was a pamphlet, *Art and Revolution* (1849), which shows how thoroughly the socialistic side of the Revolution had his sympathy and how his ideas about the regeneration of corrupt modern art were bound up with his hopes for a reformed society. Four years later the poem of *The Ring of the Nibelung* was privately printed. Anyone who believes that this poem is a work of art pure and simple and not an allegorical representation of European civilization as Wagner knew it and as he hoped it would crash to ruin, should read *Art and Revolution, The Artwork of the Future,* and some of the other essays Wagner wrote in these four years on religion, art, society, and the baleful influence of gold.

Against this background the text of *The Rhinegold* reads like a socialist tract. The third scene of the opera, with Alberich wielding the master's whip and the helpless Nibelungs mining gold in the dark shafts of Nibelheim, is a somber, frightening picture, obviously an allegory of the slaves of capitalism, the sweated labor, and the foul working conditions that did exist in many a factory and mine.

But there is more to *The Ring* than political pamphleteering and revolution. The four operas occupied Wagner's immensely fertile and acquisitive mind for more than a quarter of a century. There is everything in *The Ring,* from echoes of Marx to intimations of Freud; the gaudy, overcrowded canvases of the Viennese painter, Mackart, and the ascetic, pessimistic philosophy of Schopenhauer. From the 1848 prose *Project* to the première of the completed *Ring* at Bayreuth in 1876, conception, gestation, and birth spanned twenty-eight years, more than half of Wagner's professional career. The completed work stands as a monument to the Romantic Age, a monument of breathtaking scope and subtlety, poignance and grandeur.

As *The Divine Comedy* of Dante sums up what Henry Adams called "the thirteenth greatest of centuries," the peak of the Middle Ages, so Wagner's *Ring* epitomizes his age. Both works are rich in philosophical and political allegories. Both treat of first and last things, of basic human values, and the meaning of life itself.

Is it not curious, indeed almost uncanny, that despite the abysses of time, of geographical, cultural, and religious differences that separate the two works, the last lines of each once contained the identical key word and thought? At the end of the one hundredth canto, when Dante at last comes face to face with God, He is *"l'amor che move il sole e l'altre stelle"* ("The love which moves the sun and the other stars"). At the end of *Götterdämmerung* Brunnhilda's final words before entering the flames about to consume her and cleanse the world of guilt and corruption were to have been: *"Selig in Lust und Leid lasst die Liebe nur sein"* ("Blessed in weal or woe let there be love alone"). Eventually Wagner deleted this speech because he felt that at this point his orchestra was more eloquent than words. But the sense remained.

If there is a single central theme in Wagner's version of *The Ring* it is the conflict between love and the lust for power as symbolized by the accursed gold. When he first began seriously considering the Siegfried legend, Wagner was thirty-three years old and had been second conductor of the Dresden Royal Opera for three years. His *Rienzi, The Flying Dutchman,* and *Tannhäuser* had been produced at Dresden and he was about to begin the composition of *Lohengrin.*

Eighteen forty-eight, the year of the completion of *Lohengrin,* also brought, in rapid succession, *The Nibelungen Myth as a Project for a Drama,* then the prose scenario for *Siegfried's Death,* and finally the finished poem for *Siegfried's Death, a Grand Heroic Opera,* which corresponds to *Götterdämmerung* as we know it today.

Wagner's original intention had been to write only one opera on the Nibelungen myth, but eventually he discovered that the prehistory of *Siegfried's Death* involved too much narrative on stage. He decided to precede *Siegfried's Death* with another entire opera to be called *The Young Siegfried.* Hardly had he finished the text for *The Young Siegfried* in 1851 when he realized that two further operas would be required: *Die Walküre,* and finally *Das Rheingold,* which would go back to the beginning of the story.

This was a turning point in Wagner's life. The fantastically impractical shape his work was taking, as if it had a will and a life of its own, startled him. As a practical man of the theater,

Wagner knew there was no opera company, not even a stage, capable of producing the work as he envisaged it. But he went ahead. What courage and fanaticism this must have taken we can only try to imagine.

In a long letter to Franz Liszt, at the end of 1851, he outlined the project. A year earlier, Liszt had suggested that he might persuade the Grand Duke of Weimar to commission the composition of *Siegfried's Death* for the Weimar Opera which was under his direction. But Wagner knew that the four operas of *The Ring* would be out of the question.

It meant a great deal to Wagner when Liszt replied with the greatest enthusiasm and confidence.

"Throw yourself into it," he wrote, "and give no thought to any other consideration than your grand project, for which one could set the same program as the Cathedral Chapter of Seville gave to their architect for the construction of the Cathedral: 'Build us such a temple that future generations will say the Chapter was crazy to undertake anything so extraordinary.' And yet, there stands the Cathedral!"

The next year Wagner completed the text of *Die Walküre* and *Rheingold*. And in 1853 the entire text of *The Ring* was privately printed for distribution to a small circle of friends.

It is interesting that from the very beginning, that is in the prose *Project*, Wagner's central thought was an ethical one. The object of the rule of the gods is "ethical consciousness." But the power of the gods is based on an evil deed, the theft of the Rhinegold from Alberich. The gods can be saved from the consequences of their crime only by a free agent who will take their guilt upon himself and expiate it. It is a sort of reversal of the Christian *Agnus Dei qui tollis peccata mundi.* Instead of God (in the form of Christ) expiating the sins of mankind it is a man who must expiate the sin of the gods and thus achieve their salvation.

To this end, indeed, the gods create man, and a basic premise of *The Ring* which the casual listener is apt to overlook is that human beings are superior to the gods whom they eventually supersede. The highest aim of the gods, therefore,

becomes their own conscious desire to be destroyed and super-
seded by their own superior creation. This is all contained in
the first prose *Project*.

In the actual working out of *Siegfried's Death*, however,
Wagner did not at first embark on anything quite so compli-
cated. He ended the drama not with the destruction of the
gods but with their restoration to their primeval innocence
through the death of Siegfried, who thus expiates their guilt.
Instead of Valhalla being consumed in flames, the final tableau
showed Brunnhilda as a Valkyrie, again in full shining armor
on her horse, leading Siegfried by the hand upward to join
Wotan and the other slain heroes in Valhalla.

This optimistic and relatively simple version of things did
not last long. Wagner soon felt a need to explain what had
enabled Alberich to seize the Rhinegold in the first place. He
found the answer in his own feelings about money power.
The power to rule over men through the evil magic of gold
could be wielded only by a person who had renounced love:
not only romantic love, but love of one's fellow man, and love
as a symbol of all beneficent creative activity.

In the very first scene of *The Rhinegold*, the Rhine daughters
tell Alberich that renunciation of love will enable him to seize
the gold and make from it the ring which will give him the
power to rule the world. Alberich does so, and the melody of
the renunciation of love becomes one of the most important
leitmotifs of *The Ring*.

Wagner's sound theatrical sense led him to show Alberich
in the act of cursing love and making off with the gold. But it
was not absolutely necessary to renounce love before seizing
power. The process could be reversed: the exercise of arbitrary
power could force even a god to relinquish love against his
will. This is what happens to Wotan.

Wotan has no intention of relinquishing love. But Valhalla
is to him what the Ring is to Alberich. The inexorable price
that he has to pay for the power Valhalla confers is the sacrifice
of all he most loves: his own son, Siegmund, whose death he
causes on the battlefield; his favorite Valkyrie daughter, Brunn-

hilda, who represents his own higher nature, and whom he banishes from his sight. Even his grandson, Siegfried, is caught in the terrible consequences of Wotan's guilt, and in the end, of course, Wotan himself and all the gods are destroyed.

By July of 1857 Wagner had completed the scores of *Rheingold, Die Walküre*, and composition sketches for the first and second acts of *Siegfried*. But the prospect of a performance of *The Ring* seemed as remote as ever. He put aside *The Ring* to write *Tristan und Isolde* and *Die Meistersinger*. But he never gave up hope for *The Ring*, and in 1863 he had the full text published, together with a preface in which he expressed the hope that an art-loving German ruler would come to the rescue of the great project.

This preface was read by the Crown Prince of Bavaria, who vowed to himself that if he ever came to power he would fulfill Wagner's prayer. The very next year he came to the throne as Ludwig II, and one of his first acts was to send for Wagner, who was then in the depths of artistic disappointment and financial need. He assured Wagner that he would never again have to worry about his material support and promised him the artistic and financial means to perform the *Nibelungen* tetralogy.

Meanwhile, Ludwig put the Munich Opera at Wagner's disposal for the production of *Tristan*, which had been rejected everywhere and given up as unperformable by the Vienna Opera after fifty-seven rehearsals. The Munich première of *Die Meistersinger* followed in 1868. Finally, in 1869, Wagner resumed the composition of *Siegfried*. Five years later *Götterdämmerung* was completed, and in 1876 the first performance of the entire *Ring* cycle took place in a model theater especially for Wagner in the small Bavarian city of Bayreuth.

The fruition of Wagner's dream had cost him a bitter and exhausting struggle. Time and again King Ludwig had come to his assistance, as had on a smaller scale a legion of self-sacrificing friends and admirers. Even in the hour of triumph there were many carping, critical voices. Yet the Bayreuth festival of 1876 was a glorification of Wagner and his art, an apotheosis such as few artists, or perhaps none, have experienced in their own lifetimes.

Even Eduard Hanslick, the powerful Viennese critic, who is customarily represented as the leader of the forces of benighted opposition to Wagner, declared that Siegfried's funeral music in the last act of *Götterdämmerung* was the greatest since the *Marcia funebre* of Beethoven's *Eroica*. From across the ocean *The New York Times* sent its representative to supply, for the first time in history, cabled reviews of each night's performance for publication next morning in New York. When we realize how seldom such reviews are cabled today we have some measure of the importance which the Bayreuth achievement had even to Americans.

Within Germany, of course, a certain amount of nationalistic ballyhoo contributed to the sensation. Following so closely on the victory of the Franco-Prussian War in 1871 and the foundation of the German Empire, the Bayreuth production was regarded in many quarters as a grand manifestation of German national art. Even the unmusical German Emperor allowed himself to be persuaded that his presence was essential. But the art work of the future proved too much for him, and he left after *Die Walküre* on the second evening.

Wagner was not a nationalist in the sense of some of his supporters and visitors to Bayreuth. Hans Sachs's speech at the end of *Die Meistersinger* shows clearly enough that Wagner's nationalism was primarily a concern for German art, not for German political power.

The subject matter of *The Ring* was commonly regarded as German and had been dear to German poets and dramatists throughout the Romantic period. As early as 1810 Friedrich Heinrich Karl Fouqué, Freiherr de la Motte, wrote a Nibelungen triology called *The Hero of the North*, consisting of three epic poems: *Sigurd the Dragon Killer*, *Sigurd's Revenge*, and *Aslauga*. Fouqué also anticipated Wagner in his revival of the alliterative technique of ancient Germanic verse known as *Stabreim*.

In 1828 Ernst Raupach produced a five-act drama with

prologue called *The Nibelungen Hoard*. In 1857 Emanuel Geibel presented a drama, *Brunhild*, concerned chiefly with the romance of Brunhild and Siegfried.

In 1863 Christian Friedrich Hebbel's great dramatic trilogy *The Nibelungen* appeared. Four years later there followed a *Sigfrid and Chriemhilde* by Wegener, and one year later the *Sigfrid Sage*, the first of Wilhelm Jordan's two epic poems entitled *Die Niebelunge*. The second, *Hildebrant's Homecoming*, followed in 1874, the year of the completion of Wagner's *Götterdämmerung*. Jordan, like Fouqué and Wagner himself, revived the ancient *Stabreim*.

This alliterative technique can be illustrated by almost any page from *The Ring*. Let us take the words of Voglinda, one of the Rhine daughters in the first scene of *Das Rheingold*:

> *Nur wer der Minne*
> He who the power
>
> *Macht versagt,*
> of love forswears,
>
> *nur wer der Liebe*
> from all delights
>
> *Lust verjagt,*
> of love forbears,
>
> *nur der erzielt sich den Zauber,*
> the magic he alone can wield
>
> *zum Reif zu zwingen das Gold.*
> to forge a ring from the gold.

Minne Macht, Liebe Lust, and *erzielt . . . Zauber . . . zum . . . zwingen* are simple examples of this very flexible technique, which is capable of many variations and combinations.

Sometimes, especially when he uses very short verses and avoids the inadvertently Victorian effect of strings of flamboyant adjectives, Wagner's poetry can be extraordinarily compact and pregnant. But for the most part the poetic effects of Wagner's work lie less in his manipulation of language than in his psychological insights, the dramatic situation, and of course his music.

It is above all in music that he achieves the subtle shadings, the ambiguities, double and triple meanings, which the professional poet evokes with words alone. One of Wagner's chief devices to achieve these effects is his technique of musical allusion by means of leitmotifs, which he developed to unheard-of virtuosity.

A simple but famous example occurs in the first act of *Die Walküre,* while Siegmund is telling the story of his life. He was separated from his father in battle, he says, and never saw him again. In the orchestra we hear very, very softly the Valhalla motif. And we understand what Siegmund himself does not know—namely, that his father, who was Wotan in mortal guise, had returned to Valhalla.

In another famous scene at the very end of *Götterdämmerung* Wagner cut out some thirty lines of his text because, as he explained, the sense of the words was better communicated in the music, presumably the long orchestral close of the opera.

It was long believed, and the idea is still widespread, that Wagner, who placed such emphasis on the drama, wrote his dramatic text first and then, like other composers, set the words to music. We now know that both were conceived at once. Indeed, if either element can be said to have come first, it was the music. In the actual process of composition Wagner began his conscious work by dwelling on a certain musical mood. Out of this mood musical phrases, a rhythm, a harmony, an instrumental color would crystallize. Simultaneously fragments of dialogue took shape.

Sometimes Wagner felt that his characters began to speak of their own accord, and he tells us that in the process of composing a scene he also had the entire stage picture in mind, including the gestures and actions of the characters. Some of his earliest sketches for the plots of various works have hasty musical notations in the margin, brief memoranda to himself of the musical ideas that had been born simultaneously with the words or gestures of the drama.

There is a scene in *The Ring* which has always seemed to me to reflect this simultaneous conception of the words and music. This is set in the Hall of the Gibichungs, at the beginning of the first act of *Götterdämmerung*. The text here is taken virtually intact from the corresponding scene in *Siegfried's Death*, which, as we have seen, was written in the year of the completion of *Lohengrin*. Since musical ideas came to Wagner as he wrote down the text, it would seem logical that his original musical concept of this scene would not differ greatly in style from *Lohengrin*. And as a matter of fact, the opening of the Gibichungen scene is more wooden than is normal for the mature Wagner and closer to *Lohengrin* than to most of *Götterdämmerung*.

The rest of *Götterdämmerung*, of course, bears little resemblance to Wagner's early operas. In most scenes the orchestral texture is an almost continuous web of leitmotifs, referring back to earlier scenes of *The Ring*. And it is written with all the harmonic subtlety of a man who has *Tristan* and *Meistersinger* behind him, to say nothing of the rest of *The Ring*.

In most scenes Wagner must have replaced his original musical concept of *Siegfried's Death* with such new material. But the opening of the Gibichungen scene introduces us to three new characters who appear to have no direct dramatic or musical connection with the earlier events of *The Ring*. Here Wagner's earliest musical concept would have no competition from the more mature musical ideas of *Rheingold*, *Walküre*, and *Siegfried*. And it is quite possible that we have here a sample of the original *Siegfried's Death*.

Offhand, one would not expect research into the musical forms of a Wagner opera to throw much light on the text. But when the German musicologist, Alfred Lorenz, published the first of his four epoch-making volumes on *The Secret of Form in Richard Wagner* (Berlin, 1924) he not only gave us our first real understanding of Wagner's powerful formal structures, but he also provided additional, unarguable evidence that text and music were conceived simultaneously. Indeed, he was able to show that the whole dramatic construction is based on musical forms. *"The musical form,"* he concluded *"shapes the dramaturgical structure, and is the propelling force of the dramatic development."*

Wagner uses three basic forms. The symmetrical bow form can be represented at its simplest by the letters:

A B A

or, by more complex symmetries such as:

A B C D E D C B A

Or:

AB C AB

Rondo form consists of a recurring refrain (R) which alternates with contrasting materials:

R X R Y R Z R

The bar form, which is explained by Hans Sachs to Walter in the third act of *Die Meistersinger*, seems to have been Wagner's favorite. It consists of the repetition of an initial strain, followed by a contrasting section. This is the form of the melody of "The Star-Spangled Banner" and can be represented by the letters:

A A B

More often the two A's are not precisely alike and can be better represented as:

A A^1 B

All of these foms may be used on the most minute scale, to organize phrases within a single sentence. They may determine the shape of a short solo. At the beginning of Act Two of *Die Walküre,* for example, the famous battle cry of Brunnhilda, her "Ho-jo-to-ho," is a simple ABA bow form. In old-fashioned Italian opera this would be called a *da capo* aria. On a vaster scale, the whole first act of *Siegfried* is a freely symmetrical bow form of the ABCDCBA variety, with the Wanderer scene in the middle of the act.

We cannot go into the ramifications of Wagner's meticulous form, which is often most highly organized in passages that sound most rhapsodic and free in their expression. Often it is the musical organization of the dramatic events and dialogue that gives Wagner's stage action its peculiar theatrical force.

Though the importance of Lorenz's discoveries and of a tiny number of really original musical analyses certainly cannot be dismissed, yet the largest number of truly enlightening commentaries on Wagner have been written by non-musicians. Baudelaire's essay on *Tannhäuser,* written at the time of the *Tannhäuser* fiasco in Paris, and Nietzsche's extravagant adoration and equally extravagant rejection of Wagner in *The Birth of Tragedy from the Spirit of Music, The Case of Wagner,* and *Nietzsche contra Wagner* are among the most vivid esthetic and philosophical commentaries. Bernard Shaw's *The Perfect Wagnerite,* a witty and penetrating analysis of the story of *The Ring* as a political allegory, goes to the core of Wagner's thought from another angle. Elmer Davis's homely essay, *The Imperfect Wagnerite,* discusses *The Ring* as an allegory of the life of the well-meaning average man, and is equally convincing—and moving—on another level.

Thomas Mann, in his great essay, *The Suffering and Greatness of Richard Wagner,* describes, with enormous sensitivity and passion, not only the psychological and mythological implications of Wagner's texts, but also the poetic symbolism of such a purely orchestral passage as Siegfried's funeral music in the third act of *Götterdämmerung.*

"The overpowering accents of the music, which accompanies

Siegfried's corpse from the scene, are not intended merely for the forest boy who set out to learn what fearing is; they reveal to our emotions who is really being carried away through the descending veils of mist; the sun-god himself lies on the bier, slain by stealthy darkness; and the suggestive word comes to our aid: 'The victim of a wild boar,' Hagen says. '*He* is the accursed boar,' says Gunther, pointing to Hagen, 'who slew this hero.' The perspective opens back to the first and earliest dream pictures of mankind. Tammuz and Adonis, who were slain by the boar, Osiris, Dionysus, those who are torn and will return as the Crucified One, whose side must be pierced by a Roman spear that he may be recognized—all those who were and always are the whole world of sacrificial victims, of beauty murdered by grim winter, all are embraced in this mythical gaze—and therefore let it not be said that the creator of *Siegfried* was untrue to himself in *Parsifal*."

Among the commentators on Wagner none is more fascinating (and sometimes intentionally obscure) than Wagner himself. The Wanderer scene at the beginning of Act Three of *Siegfried* held a particular attraction for him. "We must learn how to die," he wrote to his friend August Röckel, "how to die in the complete sense of the word. Fear of the end is the source of all lovelessness, and this fear arises only when love has already begun to fade. . . .Wotan rises to the tragic grandeur of willing his own destruction. This is all we have to learn from the history of mankind: to will what is necessary and to accomplish it ourselves. The great creation of this highest self-destroying will is the final achievement of the fruitful and always-loving human being: Siegfried."

Wagner returns to this scene, with its many-faceted treatment of the theme of love, in a letter to King Ludwig concerning the resumption of work on *The Ring*. "Wonderful is the spot where . . . I shall resume the composition of the music. It is the loftiest scene of the most tragic of my heroes. Wotan, the all-powerful will to live, has resolved on his own self-sacrifice. Greater now in his renunciation than ever before in his striving, he feels omnipotent, and he calls to the Earth

Mother, Erda, the source of wisdom that once taught him to fear his end, that no fear can bind him more, since he now wills his end with the same will that used to lust only for life. His end? He knows what Erda's wisdom does not: that he lives on in Siegfried. Wotan lives on in Siegfried as every artist does in his work. The freer from traces of the artist this work is, so that the work be remembered and the artist forgotten, the more satisfied the artist is. Thus in a higher sense his being forgotten, his disappearance, his death, is the life of the work of art. These are my feelings as I turn back to the completion of my work. In order to live eternally I shall allow my Siegfried to annihilate me! Oh Blissful Death!

"With what consecration I shall awaken Brunnhilda from her long sleep! She slept while Siegfried grew to be a young man. How significant all this seems to me now! My last music was the forest birds' announcement to Siegfried that he could awaken Brunnhilda if he had not learned fear: he followed the bird, laughing, to the magic rock. That path, my royal friend—how long and hard it was for me! I thought I should never come to the rock. But if I am Wotan I shall succeed through Siegfried: he awakens the maiden, my work will live—it lives!"

EDWARD DOWNES

Foreword

Richard Wagner's four great music dramas, relating one story called *The Ring of the Nibelung*, were written for the entire world; but their message is intended to dramatize the fallacy of any attempt to conquer the world by force. The golden ring of the Nibelungs, it is said, will give its holder supreme rule on earth, but a curse is attached to this talisman forged of stolen gold, and in the end no one rules, for all are destroyed who held the cursed ring—the "eternal" gods, the simple giants, the heroic demigods, and even the poor dwarf who longed for the ring but never once touched it. Wotan's order of politics perishes from the earth (it has not yet!), and the ring goes right back to those to whom it belonged, the gliding maids of the Rhine. As the curtain descends on the doom of the gods we know that a clean sweep has been made, the earth has been cleansed and purified, and the reign of love is about to begin, with Parsifal as the representative of the *Novus Ordo Saeclorum*. Professor Köstlin well summarized the lesson of *The Ring*:

Everything, even the highest (the gods), even the noblest (Siegfried and Brunnhilda) perishes, if it allows anything to persuade it to resort to violence, either open or secret, instead of relying on Love, the only bond that holds things together.

If there was any group of people on earth who should have learned the lesson of *The Ring,* it was the German Nazis. Yet because of their amazing obtuseness, its true meaning escaped them completely. It was enough for them that Hitler loved Wagner. All that they heard in *The Ring* was the brasses.

The *Nibelungen* symbols became part and parcel of Nazi dogma. A strange fact this, but explicable perhaps by the supposition that it was their death-wish asserting itself, as was their choice of the *reversed* swastika—symbolizing *bad* luck!—as a national blazon. Hitler likened the Nazi party to Siegfried. Speaking of the first National Socialist meeting, he said: "Out of its flames was bound to come the sword which was to regain the freedom of the German Siegfried." Robert Ley, *fuehrer* of the Labor Front, carried *The Ring* imagery further. Siegfried's dragon foe was England, guardian of the hoard of *Lebensraum.* Certainly the Nazi self-identification with Siegfried was ominous, for did not this very imperfect hero meet his doom and the ring of rule he held have to be restored to its rightful owners? Just as absurd was Hitler's funeral oration delivered at Hindenburg's grave: "Departed General, enter now into Valhalla!" What a place to send a decent man! Did not *der Fuehrer* know that Valhalla, like hell in Revelation, is to be consumed in flames, and everything with it?

When the new pagan religion arose in Germany, Alfred Rosenberg, leader of the new faith, eagerly followed Hitler's will. Thus Rosenberg chose as the new god, Wotan, the "War father," who, as he stated mystically and nonsensically, "as the eternal mirror of the primeval soul forces of the nordic man, is living today as five thousand years ago." Note that in attributing eternality to Wotan the head of the Nazi religion described seriously what the composer-poet described ironically. In *The Ring* the gods call themselves "eternal," even when they discover they are mortal and that their end is near.

What an unheroic figure is the god the Nazis chose! Poor Wotan! He is only too mortal and fallible, a worried and world-weary one-eyed Wanderer, a sorry philanderer, and a henpecked husband, rejoicing only in his huge standing army of

heroes,[1] obtained by sending his illegitimate daughters, the
Valkyries, to earth to stir up war among mortals so they might
kill one another, thus giving the god the pick of the slain for
his Valhalla.

Even the shrewd Goebbels was guilty of the same folly.
"Hear *The Valkyrie* at the State Opera," he cried in simulated
ecstasy. "Wagner's sublime music is mingled with the sound
of marching of the Steel Helmet troops." As for the "sound
of marching," did not the Propaganda Minister know that the
"March" in *The Ring* is a funeral march, and that it is for
Siegfried, whom the Nazis identified with themselves?

The Nazis' love of Wagner might well have meant the kiss
of death to a lesser composer, but the most it has been able to
do is to give rise to foolish statements by certain men of music.
For instance, Carl Engels has stated: "If Hitler likes Wagner's
music, it is all the more reason why every non-Nazi should
shun and loathe it."

Wagner was the antithesis of all that the Nazis stood for. He
was anti-German, anti-national, anti-patriotic, and anti-racist.
For two years in his mid-career his dislike of his native land
was so great that in writing he refused to use the usual capital
letters. In his latter days he reverted to his earlier dislike. "No
nation is so abominable as ours," he exclaimed in an article
against vivisection. He wanted to get away from Germany and

---

[1] In giving Wotan a standing army as a plaything Wagner was
again signifying his contempt for the god. Wagner's opposition to
standing armies was lifelong. He had expressed this opposition in his
speeches and writings during the revolution of 1848, and he expressed it with equal vehemence after the Franco-Prussian War of
1870. Blaming Bismarck, he complained to Lenbach: "The whole
people is famishing, and we keep up a gigantic army to protect this
corpse. . . . The people is exhausted by constant fresh taxes, ever-
fresh augmenting of the army—it's barbaric!" Again: "Prussia and
Austria . . . are continually under arms against all Europe . . . the
consequence being a national arming which . . . exhausts the re-
sources of these two countries and establishes a military caste that is
absolutely un-German and useless . . . and inapplicable to our conditions. I do not hesitate to say that the maintenance of huge standing armies . . . will lead someday to the downfall of the monarchies."

settle in America. He was writing his *Parsifal*, he told Cosima, his wife, solely for her: "he had lost all belief in the 'German spirit.'" The journal he kept for King Ludwig expresses hatred and contempt for militaristic Prussia. While in Venice, according to Cosima's diary, "he cursed Germany, he cursed Franconia, he cursed Bayreuth." According to Newman, "Italy had filled him with a deep dislike for Germany."

No doubt his growing preoccupation with orthodox Christianity and his concentration on *Parsifal* made Wagner particularly sensitive to the growing anti-Christian and militaristic spirit springing up around him. He was alarmed at the spirit of nationalism. "This new Germany disgusts me," he wrote. It was filled with arrogant self-love:

The greater a nation is, the less importance it seems to attach to uttering its own name with this veneration. We meet much less often, in the public life of France and England, with talk about "English virtues" or "French virtues"—but the German is very much given to talking about "German depth, German earnestness, German faith," and so on.

Even good Germans possess an arrogant, warlike spirit today:

German poetry, German music, German philosophy are nowadays esteemed and honored by every nation in the world; but in his yearning after "German glory" the German, as a rule, can dream of nothing but a sort of resurrection of the Roman Empire, and the thought inspires the most good-tempered German with an unmistakable lust for mastery, a longing for the upper hand over the other nations. He forgets how detrimental to the welfare of the German peoples that notion of the Roman State has been already.

Let not the Germans think they are a great people because they have produced great men:

That Goethe and Schiller, Mozart and Beethoven have issued from the German people's womb, far too easily tempts the bulk of middling talents to consider these great minds their own by right of birth, to persuade the mass with demagogic flatulence that they themselves are Goethes and Schillers, Mozarts and Beethovens. Nothing flatters more the bent to sloth and easy-goingness than a high opinion that quite of oneself one is something great and needs take no sort of pains to first become it. This leaning is root-German, and hence no people more requires to be flicked up and compelled to help itself, to act for itself than the German. . . . It was reserved for Börne the Jew to sound the first challenge to the Germans' sloth.

However, Wagner did believe the Germans capable of the greatest things, in the future as in the past. But through culture, not war:

The Beautiful and Noble came not into the world for the sake of profit, nay, not for the sake of even fame and recognition. And everything done in the sense of this teaching is "deutsch"—and for that is the German great—and only what is done in that sense can lead Germany to greatness. . . . The German folk arrived at its rebirth . . . through its conservative temper. . . . The conquerors are the enemies of the German spirit. . . . The conquerors' brute force draws near these sciences and arts of peace, and tells them, "What of you may serve for war, shall prosper—what not, shall perish."

Not only is nationalism an error, but love of country itself is a very limited thing: "Jesus teaches us to break through the barriers of patriotism and find out our amplest satisfaction in the weal of all the human race."

The Germans do not belong to a superior race and should not claim they do. For instance: "In the French civilization the German spirit stands facing a rival equally endowed at bottom."

The Frenchman Gobineau's theories on race had impressed him for a while, but not too long, for Wagner wrote subsequently:

The blood of the Saviour, the issue from his head, his wounds upon the cross—who impiously would ask its race, if white or otherwise? Divine we call it, and its source that Godlike pity which streams through all the human species, its fount and origin. . . .

The blood of suffering mankind, as sublimated in that wondrous birth, could never flow in the interest of howsoever favored a single race; no, it sheds itself on all the human family, for noblest cleansing of man's blood from every stain. Hence the sublime simplicity of the pure Christian religion, whereas the Brahminic, for instance, applying its knowledge of the world to the insurance of supremacy for one advantaged race, became lost . . . and sank to the extreme of the absurd. Thus, notwithstanding that we have seen the blood of noblest races vitiated by admixture, the partaking of the blood of Jesus, as symbolized in the only genuine sacrament of the Christian religion, might raise the very lowest races to the purity of gods. This would have been the antidote to the decline of races through commingling, and perhaps our earthball brought forth breathing life for no other purpose than that ministrance of healing.

Germany will express its true nature when "the spirit of free manhood is loosed from the nature soil of race." At present though, nationalism, patriotism, and racism are proving a bane:

"From Herodom we have inherited nothing save bloodshed and slaughter. . . . Yet every sheer force finds a force still stronger. Therefore it cannot be an end in itself." He despised "the empty pleasure of the world-conqueror," "the positive murder of freedom . . . which so completely dominated Frederick the Great." Nor is Bismarck better, though he united the German folk—"That unity was won . . . but what it after all might mean, again was hard to answer. They tell us we shall hear someday, when much more might has been procured. German unity must first be primed to show her teeth in every quarter, even if it leaves her with nothing to chew." As a result, the nation is "the strong man armed behind locked doors, in ceaseless search for means of increase to his garnered might." There has grown "such a boundless greed of might that even the mightiest thinks he owns nothing until he has still more. What he dreams of doing with this might one seeks in vain to fathom. Everywhere we see the image of Robespierre." "The measures and actions which show us violently disposed toward the outer world can never stay without a violent reaction on ourselves." Unfortunately, "the German . . . rejoices at the harm of others." He abominated their "most inhuman use of violence when they found that nothing was to be done with human reason." [2]

Some have thought, however, that in one respect Wagner resembled Hitler and the Nazis—in anti-Semitism. But he did not. It is true that he said some stony things about the Jews; but his attitude toward them bore no resemblance to that of the Nazis, whose remedy for "the Jewish problem" was the firing squad and the gas chamber. His belief was that the Jews should cease being aliens by "uniting" with the Germans—a thought unthinkable to the men of hate, who looked upon any such assimilation into the pure German race as a crime.

Actually, Wagner was far more critical of Gentile Germans than of Jews. And the more his nation drifted into militarism and anti-Christianity the more anti-German and the less anti-Jewish did the composer become. So disgusted did he finally grow with German barbarism that he said: "It pains me, even fills me with a sense of the futility of everything I have accomplished to abandon these works to the German nation." But he had no compunctions about giving these same works to the Jews. When he wanted his most German of operas, *Die Meister-*

---

[2] The only time Wagner fell victim to the war fever was for a brief while in the course of the Franco-Prussian War. He exclaimed to Cosima that Paris deserved to be bombarded, and went so far as to write a farce satirizing the French (this weak work is much milder than Newman tries to make it). But even before the war had passed its peak, he softened, recalling the many good qualities of the French, and how amazed and delighted he had been once, hearing Beethoven played as he should be played, and as the Germans had never played him. So in his essay on Beethoven, written at the height of the conflict, he wrote in a tone of affection: "Whither our armies are now urging, there had *his* genius already begun the noblest conquest. What our thinkers, our poets, had only touched as with a half-caught word, the Beethoven symphony had stirred to its inmost core —the new religion, the world-redeeming gospel of sublimest innocence, was already understood there as by us ourselves. So let us celebrate the great path-breaker. . . . But let us celebrate him worthily, and no less worthily than the victories of German valor; for the benefactor of a world may claim still higher rank than the world conqueror."

singer, arranged for piano, he gave the job to his good Jewish friend, Carl Tausig. When he wanted his "most Christian of works," *Parsifal,* to be superbly conducted, he gave the baton to another of his good Jewish friends, Hermann Levi. And when he gave complete legal production rights to this same most Christian work and to all his other music dramas, it was to still another Jewish friend, Angelo Neumann.[3] When he invited a musician to live with him and his family at Wahnfried, the favored one was a Jew, Jacob Rubinstein.[4]

Nor would Wagner have anything to do with organized anti-Semitism. It was one thing to criticize the Jews but quite another to sign his name to a petition which might bring about their persecution. When approached by a rabid anti-Semitic organization he was shocked and would have nothing to do with them. (Although his friend, Carl von Bülow, put his name to the petition.) As Ernest Newman states with a fairness in Wagnerian matters rare for him, "Anti-Semitic in theory, Wagner was pro-Semitic in practice."[5]

---

[3] No one else was allowed to produce *Parsifal* outside Bayreuth. The letters from Wagner to Neumann show the great good will: "My dear and valued Director," "Best of Neumanns," "Dear and valued Friend," "Yours in breathless devotion," "This will take not only all your energy and capacities, but also a firm trust in the Lord—and that I feel you have. So may heaven bless you and all dependent upon you, and keep you in its sheltering care." When he heard of Wagner's death, Neumann wrote, "I felt within my soul that a god had left the earth."

[4] When the Master died, Rubinstein was utterly heartbroken.

[5] Rumors around Wagner were, and still are, that he himself was a Jew. It would have been a satisfaction, in Hitler's time, to have proved these rumors, but actually there is no evidence of their truth. Commenting on Otto Bournot's brochure, *Ludwig Heinrich Christian Geyer, der Stiefvater Richard Wagner,* Ernest Newman states:

> "Bournot has delved with Teutonic thoroughness into the records of the Geyer family, has traced it back to 1700, in which year one Benjamin Geyer was a 'town musician' in Eisleben, and has established the piquant facts that all the Geyers were of the evangelical faith, that most of them

In no sense whatever, then, was Wagner the father or proto-type of the Nazis. There was one such person, however, and he was the antithesis of Wagner. This was Friedrich Nietzsche (1844–1900), the "philosopher," who loudly advocated in his writings the rightness of might and the wrongness of Christianity. Nietzsche, actually a philology professor, and Wagner were friends till they began to understand each other's thinking, whereupon they became completely repellant to each other.

Whatever Wagner despised in Nietzsche's philosophy the Nazis rejoiced in. Pocket editions of his writings were provided for Nazi warriors, much as pocket Bibles were provided for British and American soldiers. In June 1943 Berlin Radio announced that Hitler had presented *Il Duce* with a complete set of this Antichrist's works.

If one still has doubts as to whether Wagner's thinking resembles the pseudo-thought of the "thousand-year" Reich, the following three sets of excerpts should be sufficient to dispel them.

WAGNER:

The Greek Apollo was the god of beauteous men: Jesus the God of all men; let us make all men beautiful through freedom.

Through its measureless value to the individual does the Christian religion prove its lofty mission, and that through its dogma.

---

were Protestant church organists, and that all of them married maidens of unimpeachable German extraction. It makes one smile to find how many of these alleged Jews had 'Christian' as one of their forenames, as Wagner's putative father had. Even, therefore, if it should be proved at some time or other that Geyer was Richard Wagner's real father, this can only bring with it the admission that the amount of Jewish blood in the composer's veins must have been negligibly small. At the worst he was much more of a German than, say, a semi-Dutchman like Beethoven; much more German than the present English royal family is English."

We await the fulfilment of Christ's pure teaching . . . the son of the Galilean carpenter, who preached the reign of universal human love —thus would Jesus have shown us that we all alike are men and brothers.

The very shape of the Divine had presented itself in anthropomorphic guise: it was the body of the quintessence of all pitying Love.

It was the spirit of Christianity that rewoke to life the soul of Music.

The monstrous guilt of all this life a divine and sinless being took upon himself, and expiated with his agony and death. Through this atonement all that breathes and lives should know itself redeemed.

Christianity's founder was not wise, but divine. . . . To believe in him, meant to emulate him: to hope for redemption, to strive for union with him.

. . . a lumbering philology, which fawns upon the guardians of the ancient law of the Right of the Stronger.

NIETZSCHE:

Christianity is fit for only old women and children.

How a German can even feel Christian is more than I can understand.

If humanity never gets rid of Christianity the Germans will be to blame.

Every other book becomes clean after one reads the New Testament.

The New Testament is "filthy."

Ye shall love peace as a means to new wars—and the short peace more than the long.

Ye say it is the good cause which halloweth even war? I say unto you, it is the good war which halloweth every cause.

Cruelty is one of the oldest and most indispensable elements in the foundation of culture.

I am Antichrist.

My task—one of the greatest that man could take upon himself—is to exterminate Christianity.

Incredible, Wagner has turned pious!

Richard Wagner, apparently the most complete of victors, fell suddenly, helpless and broken, before the Christian cross.

THE NAZIS:

The God of Christendom has forsaken us Germans. He is no just God. . . . The cause of our defeat was that we believed in him and abandoned our German god. (Ernst Bergmann, 1933.)

The human race is still alive, in spite of having been Christianized. (*Ibid.*, from the pagan *Twenty-five Theses.*)

The National Socialist Weltanschauung is suited only to the German race not, like the Christian, to all races. We are not out against the hundred-and-one different kinds of Christianity but Christianity itself. (From Report of Instructional Camp held by NS German Students' League, 1935.)

The Christian population of Germany notes with great perturbation that it is being ridiculed and scorned in every way in the press, theaters, lectures, and mass meetings for its faith in the will of Jesus Christ. (*Protestant Manifesto,* 1936.)

> We are the merry Hitler youth.
> We need no Christian virtue.
> For our leader, Adolf Hitler,
> Is our Redeemer, our Intercessor.
> No evil priest can stop us.
> We follow not Christ, but Horst Wessel.
> I am no Christian, and no Catholic.
> (Hitler Youth "Marching Song.")

The old Jewish shame is at last swept away;
German men, German women, beat the black priests to a jelly.
Hang them on the gallows!

Plunge the knives into the parson's body.
We'll be ready for any massacre.

Hoist the Hohenzollerns high on the lamppost!
Hurl the hand grenades into the churches!
(Fighting song forced on the students of the University of Munich.)

Wagner's relationship to the Nazis was completely antithetical. He was the prophet of their doom. Hitler, whose love for the music of Wagner was sincere, said, "Whoever wants to understand Nationalist Socialist Germany must know Wagner." Similarly, Rosenberg said, "Wagner saw the dawn of Nazism." Ironically enough, they spoke the truth. Peter Viereck stated the case succinctly. "Wagner," he said, "damned the Nazis in advance."

He had indeed. Not only parabolically, in *The Ring*, but directly, in his prose, and apparently through some superior psychic sense. Prophetically he wrote: "Is the German already tottering to his fall? . . . Woe to us and to the world if the nation itself were saved and the German folk remained but the German spirit had taken flight for the sake of power."

Then he warned: "The hardly thinkable is closer to us than we imagine."

Did he foresee Hitler too? "The German folk does not want demagogues. . . . Do we ever see a conqueror, a forcible usurper, whether folk or individual, that does not seek to found his wilful annexation on religious, mythical, or other trumped-up covenants?"

He was alarmed by the thought that a latter-day Germany would attempt to seize the accursed Ring of world rule:

To conquer new provinces, without ever considering how they are to be won over! Never to ask oneself how Holland, Switzerland, and so forth are to be converted into friends! Only the army. . . . It is not the Jews we have to complain about, for each organism tries to further its own interests.

He was particularly alarmed at the development of scientific weapons of warfare:

It can but rouse our apprehension to see the progress of the art of war departing from the springs of moral force and turning more and more to the mechanical: here the rawest forces of the lower nature powers are brought into an artificial play. . . . Already a grim and ghastly sight is offered by the armored Monitors, against which the stately sailing ship avails no more: dumb serving-men, no longer with the looks of men, attend these monsters, Art invents torpedoes for the sea, and dynamite cartouches, or the like, for everywhere else.

The weapons of war themselves may start a war:

It is thinkable that all this, with art and science, valor, point of honor, life, and chattels should one day fly into the air through some incalculable accident. . . . Then it really might look "as if God had made the world that the devil might take it."

Germany would be tinder box and sinner. Wagner wrote Konstantin Frantz that he was "convinced by historical analogies, that by the middle of the next millennium Germany would have relapsed into barbarism." According to Ernest Newman he even calculated correctly when this would be. "He estimated that our present civilization would come to an end about the middle of the twentieth century."

But Wagner was more than a prophet of doom. *Götterdämmerung* would come, but *Götterdämmerung* was not the end. Wagner looked beyond the realm of the material into a spiritual New Order of the Ages, symbolized by the Lord and Knights of the Grail. Actually, Wagner's last music drama, *Parsifal,* is the fifth and final act of *The Ring.* The composer considered it to be so. The false gods would fall, and then the knowledge of the true God would arise. After Siegfried, the hero that failed, would come Parsifal, the hero who succeeds. The earthly treasure would return to the Rhine, the heavenly treasure descend to the earth.[6] Wagner gave us no reason to doubt this interpretation. He wrote plainly of "the spiritual ascension of the Hoard into the Grail." And again: "The Nibelung's Hoard accordingly was losing more and more in material worth, to yield to a higher spiritual content." "The Grail must rank as

[6] Wagner had pictured the descent of the Grail musically as far back as Lohengrin, son of Parsifal.

the ideal representative or follower of the Nibelungen Hoard."
"The quest of the Grail replaces the struggle for the Nibelung
Hoard in Frederick's hill." This last prophecy is quite striking:
Hitler's Berchtesgaden eyrie was on the hill referred to, that of
Frederick Barbarossa.

Wagner believed in the literal prophetic truth of his story of
Parsifal. He had developed an invincible faith not only in the
divinity of Jesus, but in the virgin birth,[7] and in the healing
miracles.[8] A literal Second Coming, he believed, would follow
the downfall of the pagan order of power politics. Said he in
1878:

Can one imagine the state of barbarism at which we shall have
arrived if our social system continues for another six hundred years
or so in the footsteps of the declining Roman world dominion? I
believe that the Saviour's Second Advent, expected by the earliest
Christians in their lifetime, and later cherished as a mystic dogma,
might have a meaning for that future date, and perchance amid
occurrences not totally unlike those sketched in the Apocalypse. For
in the conceivable event of a relapse of our whole culture into
barbarism we may take one thing for granted: namely, that our historical science, our criticism and chemistry of knowledge would
also have come to an end; whilst it may be hoped, on the contrary,

[7] "In the history of Christianity we certainly meet repeated in-
stances of miraculous powers conferred by pure virginity, where a
metaphysical concurs very well with a physiologic explanation."

[8] Wagner reasoned that since the material world is "null, an opti-
cal delusion," we must "seek the only Truth beyond it," which will
upset so-called material law. In union with God, man is "of super-
human power." So intense was Wagner's Christianity that its expression in *Parsifal* overwhelmed Nietzsche, who wrote: "Has Wagner ever written anything better? . . . It has an extraordinary sublimity
of feeling . . . of loftiness in the most startling sense of the word, of
a cognizance and a penetration of vision that cuts through the soul as
with a knife, of sympathy with what is seen and shown forth. We get
something comparable to it in Dante, but nowhere else. . . . I cannot
think of it without feeling violently shaken, so elevated was I by it,
so deeply moved. It was as if someone were speaking to me again,
after many years, about the problems that disturb me—naturally not
supplying the answers I would give, but the Christian answer."

that theology would by then have come to a final agreement with the Gospels, and the free understanding of Revelation be opened to us without Jehovaistic subtleties—for which event the Saviour promised us his coming back.[9]

[9] One sometimes wonders if Wagner's religious thinking was not moving slowly and inexorably toward Catholic Christianity. Despite his antagonism to priestcraft, which he maintained to the end of his days, his religious orthodoxy was growing, taking in not only the divinity of Christ, the virgin birth, and the Second Coming, but ritual and dogma. And in a very late essay he describes with rapture the ecstasy he feels when viewing artistic reproductions of the Madonna and Child.

STEWART ROBB

Translator's Note

There has long been a need for a new and representative translation of Wagner's great epic poem, which, apart from its music, is a classic of world literature, though not available as such in English. Translations there have been, intended to be both readable and singable, but at their best such translations have been poor, and at their worst ludicrous.

A few samples from available standard translations of the tetralogy will prove the point more quickly than many words. For instance, in *Die Walküre*, Wotan, explaining to his wife Fricka that he has no influence over Siegmund, says: "His weird he shall dree." That is, Siegmund shall undergo his destiny. How much clearer is Wagner than his translator Meltzer: "*Er geh' seines Weg's.*" Here is a deliberate reaching out for obscurity on the part of the translator where the original text is completely clear.

In the same music drama Wotan informs Brunnhilda of the magic sword carried by Siegmund:

> *Ein Sieg-Schwert*
> *Schwingt Siegmund.*

This, in the standard Corder version, becomes

> *A sooth-sword*
> *Swings Siegmund.*

Need one say more? These are current translations, still available in librettos and in piano scores. Yet one of them is so ancient (the Corder version) as to have been disapproved of by Wagner himself!

My own approach has been to translate *The Ring* into clear, understandable modern English, avoiding obscurities of expression and archaic words such as *eke, erst, hight,* and so on, yet preserving the rhythms of the original German where possible, and even some of the alliterative effects. The words of my translation have at all times been carefully fitted to Wagner's vocal lines.

At any rate, here is a new English version of *Der Ring des Nibelungen* which can be enjoyed by the general reader as well as sung on the opera stage. This version keeps close to the meaning of the original text of Wagner, closer perhaps than previous translations. Withal it does not sound like a translation, but as though originally written in English. A reading aloud will show this.

S. R.

THE RHINEGOLD

CHARACTERS

WOTAN
DONNER
FROH
LOGE

Gods

FASOLT
FAFNER

Giants

ALBERICH
MIME

Nibelungs (Gnomes)

FRICKA
FREIA
ERDA

Goddesses

VOGLINDA
VELLGUNDA
FLOSSHILDA

Rhine-Daughters

1

THE RHINEGOLD

FIRST SCENE

At the Bottom of the Rhine

Greenish twilight, lighter above, darker below. The upper part of the scene is filled with moving water. Toward the ground the waters distill into a fine mist which flows like a train of clouds over the gloomy depths. Everywhere steep points of rock jut up, while the ground is a confusion of jagged pieces, with no place level.

Round a rock whose peak rises into the lighter water, a Rhine-nymph is seen swimming.

VOGLINDA.

> Weia! Waga!
> Lull us, you waters,
> cradle and rock us!
> Wagalaweia!
> Wallala weiala weia!

VELLGUNDA'S
VOICE. *(from above)*

> Voglinda, are you on guard?

VOGLINDA.

> Alone, till our Vellgunda comes.
> *(diving from the surface to the reef)*

VELLGUNDA.

> Let's see how you watch.

3

VOGLINDA.
(avoiding her by swimming)

> Out of your reach!
> *(They seek playfully to catch each other.)*

FLOSSHILDA'S
VOICE. *(from above)*

> Heiala weia!
> Hey, you wild sisters!

VELLGUNDA.

> Flosshilda, swim!
> Voglinda flees!
> Help me to capture our sister!

FLOSSHILDA.
(diving down)

> You guard the gold
> badly today!
> Watch with more care
> the slumberer's bed,
> else both will pay for your play!

> *(The two separate with merry cries. Floss-
> hilda chases first one, then the other. They
> evade her, then unite to pursue her in turn.
> Darting about like fish from rock to rock they
> laugh and sport.*

> *From a dark chasm Alberich clambers up to
> one of the rocks. He halts in a shadow and
> watches the nymphs with increasing delight.)*

ALBERICH.

> Ho, ho, you nixies!
> What an enchanting,
> delicate folk!
> From Nibelhome's night
> welcome a guest
> who'd like to come near.
> *(The girls leave off playing.)*

VOGLINDA.

> Hey! who is there?

FLOSSHILDA.

> It's dark and it speaks!

VOGLINDA.

> Look out for the spy!
> *(They dive down deeper to perceive the*
> *Nibelung.)*

VOGLINDA &
VELLGUNDA.

> Pfui! a nasty imp!

FLOSSHILDA.
(darting upward)

> Look to the gold!
> *(The others follow her, and all three quickly*
> *gather round the central rock.)*
> Father warned us
> of such a foe.

ALBERICH.

> Hey, you up there!

THE THREE GIRLS.

> What's up with you, down there?

ALBERICH.

> Would I disturb your play
> if I stood and watched?
> Dive to me downward.
> This poor Nibelung
> would love to be romping with you!

VOGLINDA.

> He wishes to join us?

VELLGUNDA.

> Surely he jokes?

ALBERICH.

> How fair and bright
> in the light you seem!
> I'd like to put my arm
> round your delicate waist—
> if you'd kindly come down!

FLOSSHILDA.

> My fear has all gone!
> The foe is in love!
>
> *(They laugh.)*

VELLGUNDA.

> Lascivious owl!

VOGLINDA.

Let us approach him!
*(She lets herself to the peak of the rock, at
the foot of which Alberich is.)*

ALBERICH.

She's coming down here!

VOGLINDA.

Now try to come near.

ALBERICH.
*(clambers with gnomelike nimbleness, but with difficulty, to
the point of the rock)*

What a slimy,
slippery surface!
I slide and slip!
My hands and my feet
cannot find any place
that is good to support me.
Muggy dampness
fills up my nostrils.

(Sneezes.)

Accursed sneezing!
(He has approached Voglinda.)

VOGLINDA.
(laughing)

See how finely
my love can sneeze!

ALBERICH.
(trying to clasp her)

O, be my dear,
you womanly child!

VOGLINDA.
(eluding him)

If you would woo,
then woo me up here!

ALBERICH.
(scratching his head)

Alas! You don't stay!
Come once more here!
Hard for me—
what is easy for you.

VOGLINDA.
(swinging down to a third rock in the depths)
> Clamber down here,
> then grip me quite firmly.

ALBERICH.
> Much better down lower.
>> *(She darts up to a rock at the side.)*

VOGLINDA.
> But now I am higher!
>> *(The nymphs all laugh.)*

ALBERICH.
> Just how shall I catch
> this scary fish?
>> *(He hastily clambers after her.)*
> Wait a bit, false one!

VELLGUNDA.
(has descended to a low rock on the opposite side)
> Heia, my fine one!
> Can you not hear?

ALBERICH.
(turning around)
> O, did you call?

VELLGUNDA.
> I caution you well,
> just come here to me:
> keep from Voglinda!

ALBERICH.
(while he hastily clambers over the rocky ground toward Vellgunda.)
> You're fairer far
> than that one who's shy.
> Her form's less shining,
> and much too smooth.
> Just dive down deeper,
> if you would reach me.

VELLGUNDA.
(descending a little)
> So now am I near?

ALBERICH.
> Not yet enough!
> Just twine your slender arms

about me,
that I may fondle
your neck with my fingers,
and tenderly, ardently,
press myself close to your bosom!

VELLGUNDA.

Are you in love,
and pining for kindness?
Let's see, you beauty,
just what you can show!
Pfui! you hunchbacked,
horrible gawk!
Swarthy, scurvy
and sulphurous dwarf!
(Alberich tries to detain her by force.)
Look for a sweetheart
like to yourself!

ALBERICH.

Although I'm not cute,
I'll capture you fast!

VELLGUNDA.
(darting up to the central rock)
Quite fast,
or else I'll be gone.

VOGLINDA &
FLOSSHILDA. *(laughing)*
Ha ha ha ha ha ha!

ALBERICH.
(calling angrily after Vellgunda)
Lying child!
Bony, frostbitten fish!
Am I not lovely,
dainty and pleasant,
smooth and bright!
Get eels for your lovers,
if you find my skin foul!

FLOSSHILDA.

Why scold so, imp?
Why be cast down?
You've wooed only two—

ask now the third one:
one quite sweet
promises sweet reward!

*seduction-
false*

ALBERICH.

That's a song
good for my ears!
How fine to find
more than just one.
I think I'll please one out of many—
with one though, none of them wants me!
Let me believe you:
so come here below!

FLOSSHILDA.
(dives down to Alberich)

How foolish are
my stupid sisters
not to find you quite fair!

ALBERICH.
(approaching her hastily)

How dull and base
seems all that they are,
compared to the charms that are yours.

FLOSSHILDA.

O, sing right on
in gentle tone;
your voice seduces my ears!

ALBERICH.
(touching her caressingly)

I shake, thrill,
and flutter at heart,
hearing your honey-sweet praise.

FLOSSHILDA.

How your attractiveness
joys my eyes!
With your gentle smile
you inspire my soul!
                    (drawing him tenderly to her)
Blessedest man!

ALBERICH.

Sweetest of maids!

FLOSSHILDA.

Were you but mine!

ALBERICH.

Be mine for ever!

FLOSSHILDA.

O! your piercing old glance,
and your bristly old beard,
to see them and feel them forever!
That your flourishing locks
of porcupine hair
might float round Flosshilda always!
With your form like a toad,
and your voice like a croak,
O, might I, mute and amazed,
only see and hear these!

VOGLINDA &
VELLGUNDA.

Ha ha ha ha ha ha!

ALBERICH.
(timidly)

Are you laughing at me?

FLOSSHILDA.
(suddenly tearing herself from him)

How fitting an end to the song!
*(She darts up to her sisters and joins them in
their laughter.)*

ALBERICH.
(with screaming voice)

Woe's me! Ah, woe's me!
Alas! Alas!
The third one, so dear,
betrays me as well?
You shocking, wily,
wicked, disorderly riff-raff!
Brood of the nixies,
treacherous breeders of lies!

VOGLINDA,
VELLGUNDA &
FLOSSHILDA.

Walala! Lalaleia! Lalei!
Heiaha! Heia! Haha!

Shame on you, elf-man,
scolding down yonder!
Take the counsel we tender!
Just why, you faint-heart,
did you not tie
the lady that you love?
True are we,
free of deceit
to wooers when we're caught.
Capture us, then,
and have no more fear,
for our speed is slow in the waves.
*(They swim about, hither and thither, high
and low, to incite Alberich to pursuit.)*

ALBERICH.

Right through my limbs
there rages a fire
which burns and glows!
Wrath and ardor,
wild and mighty,
rake up my spirit!
Though you may laugh and lie,
passion urges me on,
And one must yield to my lusting.
*(He pursues them with desperate efforts,
clambering from rock to rock, springing from
one to another, and striving to reach first one
nymph and then another, while they always
escape him with merry cries. He staggers,
falls below, and then climbs up hastily again,
undaunted. They descend a little lower. At
last, his patience exhausted, he pauses breathless and shakes his fist at them.)*
One only in my grip!
*(He remains in speechless rage gazing up-
ward, when suddenly he is riveted to the
spot, for through the water above breaks an
ever-increasing glow, which on the summit
of the central rock kindles gradually to a
blinding yellow gleam; a magical golden light
then streams from thence through the water.)*

VOGLINDA.

> Look, sisters!
> The wakener laughs in the deep.

VELLGUNDA.

> Through dark green surge
> he calls the blest sleeper to wake.

FLOSSHILDA.

> He kisses her <u>eyelids</u>,
> so they will <u>open.</u>   *see = gold*

VELLGUNDA.

> See her smiling
> with gentle light!

VOGLINDA.

> Through the darkling waves
> shines our radiant star!

ALL THREE GIRLS.

> Heiajaheia!
> Heiajaheia!
> Walalalalaleia jahei!
> Rhinegold!
> Rhinegold!
> Luminous joy,
> your laugh is so bright and rare!
> Noble the gleam
> that radiantly pierces the waves!
> Heiajahei!
> Heiajaheia!
> Waken, friend!
> Wake in joy!
> Rapturous games
> we'll gambol with you:
> look at the flash
> lighting the flood.
> We float around diving,
> dancing and singing,
> and bathe in your glorious bed!
> Rhinegold
> Rhinegold!
> Heiajaha!
> Walalaleia jahei!

ALBERICH.
(whose eyes, fascinated by the light, are fixed on the gold)

> What is it, you sleek ones,
> so gleams and glows up there?

ALL THREE GIRLS.

> Have you not heard, you poor lout,
> of the Rhinegold? Where were you born?

VELLGUNDA.

> The imp knows not
> of the gold's bright eyes, then,
> which wake and sleep, by turns?

VOGLINDA.

> Of the wondrous star
> that gleams in the deep,
> and nobly brightens the surge?

ALL THREE GIRLS.

> See how sweetly
> we glide in its glances!
> If you, faint-heart,
> would bathe in glory,
> then swim and revel with us.

> *(They laugh.)*

ALBERICH.

> If the gold is worthless
> except when you play,
> I surely don't want it!

VOGLINDA.

> You would not scorn
> gold of this kind
> if you knew of its wonders.

VELLGUNDA.

> And world-rule is
> the prize of the one
> who out of the Rhinegold
> fashions a ring
> imparting a measureless might.

FLOSSHILDA.

> Our father said it,
> and strictly bade us
> guard the treasure

with cunning care,
that no swindler might greedily filch it.
So peace, you gossiping crew!

VELLGUNDA.

O, clever sister,
you're blaming us both!
Do you not know
who is allowed
to use the gold as he will?

VOGLINDA.

He who forswears
the power of love,
he who forswears
the joys of love:
that man alone finds the magic
to forge the gold to a ring.

VELLGUNDA.

Why then, we are safe,
and need not fear,
for love rules all that's living:
nothing that lives flees affection.

VOGLINDA.

And least of all he,
the lecherous imp,
who's nearly dead
panting for love.

FLOSSHILDA.

I fear not him,
and I'm one to know
I was nearly scorched,
he was so hot.

VELLGUNDA.

A brimstone brand
in the surging wave!
A lovesick passion
hissing aloud!

ALL THREE GIRLS.

Walala! Walaleialala!
Loveliest elf-man!
Can't you laugh too?

In the golden shimmer
how radiant you seem!
O come, lovely one,
join in our laugh!
*(They laugh and sing, swimming up and
down in the glow. Alberich's eyes are riveted
on the gold.)*

ALBERICH.

So earth's kingdom
is mine to possess just through you?
If love be denied me,
yet pleasure is mine, if I'm smart!
(Very loud)

Mock as you will,
the Nibelung's near to your toy!
*(Raging, he springs to the central rock and
climbs it. The girls separate screaming and
dart up in different directions.)*

ALL THREE GIRLS.

Heia! Heia! heiahahei!
Save yourselves!
The imp is quite mad!
How the water spurts
where he has sprung!
His love has made him insane!
(They laugh wildly.)

ALBERICH.

Now do you fear?
Make love in the darkness,
fishified race!
(He reaches a greedy hand toward the gold.)
Your light now shall be quenched:
I'll plunder the guarded gold,
forging the ring of revenge.
So hear this, you waves:
I renounce love, and curse it!

*(With terrible strength he tears the gold from
the rock and, hastily descending, disappears
below. Sudden darkness falls. The nymphs
dive down after the robber.)*

THE THREE GIRLS.
(screaming)

> Capture the robber!
> Rescue the gold!
> Help us! Help us!
> Woe! Woe!

(The flood falls with them into the deep. Far below is heard Alberich's mocking laughter. Black waves seem to cover all.)

SECOND SCENE

Gradually the waves give place to clouds which clear off in fine mist, revealing

An Open Space on a Mountaintop

The dawning day lights up with growing luster a castle with glittering pinnacles, which stands on a cliff in the background: between this and the foreground is a deep valley through which the Rhine flows. At one side Wotan, king of the gods, and Fricka his wife are lying asleep in a flowery mead.

FRICKA.
(wakes, and her eyes light on the castle. She gives a start.)
> Wotan, my lord! Awaken!

WOTAN.
(still dreaming)

> My hall of blessed delight
> is guarded at door and gate.
> Manhood's honor,
> infinite might,
> towers to endless renown!

FRICKA.
(shaking him)

> Up from your dreams
> of rosy deceit!
> Awaken, lord, and consider!

> *(Wotan wakes and raises himself a little. His eyes are immediately riveted on the castle.)*

WOTAN.

The glorious work is achieved!
The gods' own castle
on mountain height!
Wondrous walls
of glittering pomp,
as I planned in my dream—
just the way I desired!
Strong and fair,
see how it looms:
lofty, lordly abode!

FRICKA.

The joy you fashion
gives me alarm.
You love your hall:
my fears are for Freia!
Heedless one, try to remember
the price that has to be paid!
The castle's ready,
the payment is due.
Remember well what you pledged.

WOTAN.

I mind well what they demanded,
I tamed them by
the bargain I made,
so that they built
the noblest of castles.
It stands now—thanks to the giants.
And the price? Think not of that.

FRICKA.

Outrageous, laughable lightness!
Cheerful, hardhearted folly!
Had I but known of your deal,
I might have hindered the fraud,
the men though, in scorn
kept away from the women
—without confiding in us—
to talk all alone with the giants.
So without shame
you willingly

gave them Freia, my beautiful sister,
in this villainous deal!
What can you menfolk
see holy and good
once you're greedy for power!

WOTAN.

Did not Fricka
harbor such greed
herself when she craved for the hall?

FRICKA.

But I wished you faithful and true,
and sadly had to worry
how to keep you beside me
when you would stray far from home.
Halls great and lofty,
warm, household order—
these might entice you
to tarry at home.
But you in your fort
could think of only arms and war:
all to enhance
lordship and power.
And yet your majestical castle
but stands as a cradle of strife.

WOTAN.
(smiling)

If you would keep me
confined in my fastness,
you yet must grant to my godhood
that, in the castle's confines
still I may conquer the world that's
        without.
Wandering and change
are loved by all.
I too must have some amusement!

FRICKA.

Aggravating,
hardhearted man!
For the idle toys
of lordship and might

you'd gamble away in contempt
love and a woman's worth?

WOTAN.

That time I wooed you to win you
I won by wager,
with an eye as the risk.
How foolish then to complain!
Women I honor,
still more than you like!
I'll never abandon
Freia the good.
I never held such a thought.

FRICKA.
(looking away in anxious expectation)

Then save her right now:
her helpless distress
brings her here running.

(Freia enters, as if in flight.)

FREIA.

Help me, sister!
Save me, O, Wotan!
The giant scared me
near the great mountain,
and now he's coming to catch me.

WOTAN

Let him threat!
Have you seen Loge?

FRICKA.

Tell me, why do you trust
in the treacherous god?
He's hurt us much through his tricks.
I see no end to his fooling.

WOTAN.

Where honest strength serves
I ask no one for counsel.
But to turn the hate
of foes to profit
needs both cunning and skill,—
a talent that Loge knows well.

He who arranged me this pact
has pledged the ransom for Freia.
I firmly trust in his skill.

FRICKA.

And he leaves you alone.
The giants now
are striding this way,
so where's your cunning ally?

FREIA.

Just what delays my brothers
from helping their sisters,
since my kinsman refuses to help?
O help me, Donner!
Hither, hither!
Rescue Freia, my Froh!

FRICKA.

Through their wicked deal they betrayed
        you,
and now they hide from your sight.

(*Fasolt and Fafner, men of gigantic stature,
        armed with long staves, enter.*)

FASOLT.

Soft sleep
sealed your eyes,
while we,
the sleepless workers, built your walls.
Mighty toil
tired us not.
Heavy stones
were heaped by us.
Towers rose,
doors and gates,
and at last
your fair and stately halls.
                    (*pointing to the castle*)

There stands
what we built you,
shimmering bright
in light of day.

Enter in,
but pay our wage.

WOTAN.

Men, tell us your price.
What payment was agreed on?

FASOLT.

Agreed was
what we thought would be fair:
—Your memory is dull!—
Freia, the lovely,
Holda, the gracious.
The wage is this.
We're taking her home.

WOTAN.
(*quickly*)

What is this?
Are you out of your mind?
Ask for something else.
Freia is not up for sale.

FASOLT.

What *is* this? Ha!
Up to a trick?
Betraying your word?
What your spear holds,
is it in jest—
all those words of truth to bargains?

FAFNER.

Most trusting brother,
any fool knows he's false.

FASOLT.

Son of light,
light of honor,
hear, and heed yourself.
In bargains keep your word!
What you are,
are you only through treaties,
and all your might
well defined and precise.
More wise are you
than we are clever,

since you have bound us
to keep the peace.
Yet I must curse your wisdom.
Peace shall flee far from Wotan,
when you don't frankly,
fairly uphold
the terms of your contracts in truth!
A stupid giant
tells you this;
you wise one, take it from him!

WOTAN.

How sly you are to take for truth
what was told you in jesting!
The goddess is lovely,
light and fair—
what use have dolts for her charms?

FASOLT.

Must you flout?
Ha, how unjust,
you, who through beauty rule,
shimmering, radiant race!
Like fools you strive
for your towers of stone,
bartering for the work
glorious woman in pledge!
We doltheads drudge away,
sweating with callous-hard hands
to earn us a woman,
who'll grace with her charm the
homes of poor devils—
and you say all was a jest!

FAFNER.

Hush your stupid chatter,
no prize comes from this deal.
Freia's charms help little.
It's much, though,
to seize her from the immortals.
Golden apples
grow and bloom in her garden.
She alone

knows the apples and tends them.
This goodly fruit
grants to her clansfolk
an endless youth
time cannot wither.
Sick and pale,
their beauty will vanish.
Soon they'll pass,
old and worn out
if their Freia is taken.
So I say we should carry her off!

WOTAN.
(to himself)

Loge waits too long!

FASOLT.

So, what shall it be?

WOTAN.

Ask another wage.

FASOLT.

No other: Freia alone!

FAFNER.

You there, follow us!
*(Fafner and Fasolt press toward Freia. Froh
and Donner rush in.)*

FREIA.

Help! Help from the hard-hearts!

FROH.
(clasping Freia in his arms)
To me, Freia!

(to Fafner)

Off with you, villain!
Froh guards the fair one!

DONNER.
(placing himself between the two giants)
Fasolt and Fafner,
What do you know
of my hammer's mighty blows?

FAFNER.

What threat is this?

FASOLT.

Why break in here?

>Strife's not of our choice,
>we only want what we've earned.

DONNER.
(swinging his hammer)

>I've given many
>giants their pay.
>Come here! A weighty wage
>dealt in full measure is due.

WOTAN.
(interposing his spear between the adversaries)

>Halt, you wild man!
>Nothing through force!
>All deals are kept
>through my sacred spear.
>Spare then your hammer's blow!

FREIA.

>Sorrow! Sorrow!
>Wotan forsakes me!

FRICKA.

>Is this your intent,
>terrible man?

WOTAN.
(turning, he sees Loge coming)

>Loge, finally!
>Now you make haste,
>thinking to straighten
>the sorry business you handled?

LOGE.
(ascending from the valley)

>What? just what business
>was it I handled!
>Was it when you bargained
>with the giants that time?
>I'm driven by whim
>to height and to depth.
>House and hearth
>attract me not.
>Donner and Froh
>have hankered for roof and rooms.
>If they would woo,

a house first
they must own.
A lordly hall, a castle brave,
these have made Wotan's wish.
Roof and court,
tower and hall,
that blessed abode—
it stands now firm and sound.
I checked the lordly
walls myself
and all was sound,
perfectly made.
Fafner and Fasolt
kept to their word:
no stone's loose in the joints.
Nor was I idle,
like many here.
He lies, who says that I was!

WOTAN.

Slyly you'd soften me up.
Try not to trick me,
stick to the facts as they are!
Of all the gods,
it was I alone
brought you as friend
to the crew that trusted you not.
Speak and show your skill!
The time the builders required
and asked Freia in payment,
you knew the reason
why I agreed:
because you solemnly promised
to ransom the glorious pledge.

LOGE.

I said I'd do
some careful thinking
how to redeem it.
Yes, that I recall.
But, to discover

what never was
nor yet can be,
how could I make such a promise?

FRICKA.
(to Wotan)

See what kind of a
rascal you trust!

FROH.

Though you're Loge,
a better name's liar!

DONNER.

Accursed fire,
I'll put you out!

LOGE.

Just to mask your errors,
you scold me, blockheads!
(Donner and Froh threaten him.)

WOTAN.
(warning them off)

Take care, don't bother my friend!
You know not Loge's art.
Rich advice
comes from his lips,
when we wait for his words.

FAFNER.

No more waiting:
quick, our wage!

FASOLT.

We've waited too long!

WOTAN.
(to Loge)

Now hark, stubborn one!
Keep your word!
Why wander round here and there?

LOGE.

I always meet
ingratitude!
Concerned for your sake,
hoping to help,
I scouted around

to the ends of the earth.
I sought a ransom for Freia
such as the giants might like.
I sought vainly,
and plainly now see
in the whole wide world
nothing's so hard
to replace in heart of a man
as woman's sweetness and worth!
(All exhibit surprise and various emotions.)
I asked everything living
in water and earth and air,
this question,
ever inquiring,
where nature puts forth,
and seedlings are stirring:
what does a man
hold mightier still
than woman's beauty and worth?
But in all places I went to,
my cunning question
was greeted with laughs.
In water, earth and air
female and love
are all their care.
Just one I met with
had really cast love aside,
He gave it up
for sake of some ruddy gold.
The Rhine's bright-gleaming children
clamored woe in my ears.
The Nibelung,
Night-Alberich,
courted the girls,
hoping for grace, but in vain.
The Rhinegold he
robbed them in thievish revenge.
He thinks it now
the worthiest good,
greater than woman's grace.

For their glittering toy,
thus torn from the deep,
the daughters make such lamenting,
To you, Wotan,
turning in prayers
to let justice fall on the robber,
and so return
their treasure to them,
to rest in their waters forever.
This I promised
to speak of to Wotan,
and this has Loge performed.

WOTAN.

You are either
a fool or deceiver!
I'm in trouble myself,
how can I help someone else?

FASOLT.
(to Fafner)

I grudge giving gold to Alberich.
He's done much damage already.
His cunning, though,
has kept him safely out of our clutch.

FAFNER.

New despite
will come from the dwarf—
now gold has brought him power.
You there, Loge,
say without lies
what power is lodged in this gold
that it satisfies the dwarf.

LOGE.

A toy merely,
within deep waters,
serving the children for sport.
Yet when it is fashioned
into
a circlet
it will give highest power
and grant its owner the earth.

WOTAN.
(thoughtfully)

> I have heard
> some rumors about it:
> runes of riches
> hide in its ruddy gleam.
> Boundless power
> and wealth will the ring bestow.

FRICKA.
(softly to Loge)

> Would the golden trinket
> make some glittering gear
> for women to wear in show?

LOGE.

> A wife would keep
> her husband quite true
> could she but win
> the trick of that gold,
> so brightly forged by Nibelungs,
> servants and slaves to the ring.

FRICKA.
(coaxingly to Wotan)

> I wish that my lord
> could come by the gold!

> *(Wotan appears more and more bewitched
> with his thought.)*

WOTAN.

> Control of that circlet
> might be wise, to my thinking.
> Yet how, Loge,
> could it be done—
> how shape the thing for my ends?

LOGE.

> Some rune of magic
> makes the gold a ring.
> No one knows it.
> It's easy though to learn
> by him who forswears love.
> *(Wotan turns away discouraged.)*
> That suits you not—

too late for you, too.
Alberich wasted no time.
Fearless, he won
the magic's might:
success was his with the ring.

DONNER.
(to Wotan)

We should wrest
the ring from the dwarf,
else we will all be his servants.

WOTAN.

That ring I must capture!

FROH.

Now it's easy
to win without cursing love.

LOGE.
(harshly)

Quite easy,
it's child's play—no art required!

WOTAN.

Advise us, how?

LOGE.

By theft!
What a thief stole,
that steal from the thief.
How easy to come by one's own!
Yet the Nibelung
is skilled in wicked aims.
What you do
has to be clever,
if you'd overcome the thief,
so the Rhine-god's daughters
may have their ruddy gold
once more to play with—
for which they're crying to you.

WOTAN.

The Rhine-god's daughters?
What nonsense is this?

FRICKA.

Oh, that watery brood

makes me offended:
for many men—
I'm sad to say—
have perished, allured to their bath.

FAFNER.
(to Fasolt)

Trust me, glittering gold
like that is better than she.
Besides, the magical gold
brings eternal youth with its power.
Hear, Wotan, our very last words!
Let your Freia remain here.
Smaller payment
now will suit us.
We clumsy giants want
only gold of the Nibelung hoard.

WOTAN.

Have you gone mad?
Just how can I grant you
what is not mine yet, you rascals?

FAFNER.

Hard work went
into that fort.
Quite simply,
with cunning control
(which our might could never achieve)
you'll fetter the Nibelung fast.

WOTAN.

For *you* should I
bother with Alberich?
For *you* fetter the foe?
Unashamed,
with all too much greed,
my kindness turned you to clowns!

FASOLT.
(suddenly seizes Freia and draws her to one side with Fafner)

This way, girl!
You're in our power!
Just come, you are our pledge
till the ransom arrives.

FREIA.
(shrieking)

Help me! Save me! Woe!

FAFNER.

We shall take her
far from here!
Till evening, mark me well—
know, she stands as a pledge.
We're coming back, though,
so wait for us,
and unless you give in ransom
the Rhinegold fair and red—

FASOLT.
(interrupting)

The time will be ended,
Freia will leave you
as ours, and never come back.

FREIA.
(crying out)

Sister! Brothers!
Save me! Help!
*(She is dragged away by the hastily retreating
giants.)*

FROH.

After her, quick!

DONNER.

Everything's ruined!
(They look inquiringly at Wotan.)

FREIA.
(in the distance)

Save me! Help!

LOGE.
(looking after the giants)

Over stick and stone they stride
down through the vale.
Through the shallows of the Rhine
see how they are wading.
Freia hangs,
sad, joyless,
upon the backs of the roughnecks!
Heia! Hi!

The blockheads are stumbling along!
There they stalk, right through the vale.
(He turns to the gods.)

What thought makes Wotan so wild?
Alas, what's ailing the gods?
*(A pale mist, that grows denser and denser,
fills the air. As they stand in it, the gods seem
to become wan and aged. Alarmed, they
watch Wotan, who is gazing thoughtfully at
the ground.)*

Is there a mist here?
You've grown so withered,
fearful and pale,
and the bloom has fled your cheeks.
The light of your eyes has gone out!
Quick, my Froh!
Day is still young!
From your hand, Donner,
the hammer is falling!
What's wrong with Fricka?
Can she be grieving
at Wotan's gloomy decline
that makes him suddenly old?

FRICKA.

Woe's me! Woe's me!
What has gone wrong?

DONNER.

My hand has sunk!

FROH.

My heart has stopped!

LOGE.

I have it! Learn what you're lacking!
You've had no taste
of Freia's fine apples today.
The golden apples
from out her garden
have kept you all hearty and young—
eating them every day.
The gardener's guardian
has now been kidnaped.

On the branches starves
and dries the fruit.
You'll soon see it decay.
My worry is less,
for Freia was always
stingy with me,
grudging the exquisite fruit.
For all I have
is half of the lineage of gods.
Yet you trusted wholly
to the apples of youth.
The giants perceived this well.
They got together,
plotting your death.
So give thought to your defense.
Lacking the apples,
old and gray,
sad and sullen,
shriveled, a scorn to the world,
the race of gods must cease.

FRICKA.
(*in dread*)

Wotan, my lord!
Unhappy man!
See how your light
and frivolous thoughts
have brought us shame and scorn!

WOTAN.
(*starting up with sudden resolution*)

Up, Loge,
and off with me!
We now must descend to the Nibelungs!
I'm going to ravish the gold.

LOGE.

The Rhine-daughters
called for your help,
so may they expect restitution?

FRICKA.

Quiet, babbler!
Freia, the noble,

Freia now must be rescued

LOGE.

As you command,
so shall I lead.
Shall we go
down by the way of the Rhine?

WOTAN.

Not through the Rhine!

LOGE.

We'll swing ourselves
right through the brimstone.
Just slip that way with me now!
(*He goes ahead and disappears at the side
down a crevice, from which immediately a
sulphurous vapor rises.*)

WOTAN.

You others, wait
till evening here.
Our youth that left us
returns when I ravish the gold.
(*He clambers after Loge into the cleft. The
sulphurous vapor increases.*)

DONNER.

Fare you well, Wotan!

FROH.

Good luck! Good luck!

FRICKA.

O come back soon
to her who's afraid.

(*The sulfurous vapor thickens to a black cloud. This changes
to solid dark rocky chasms, which also move upward. From
various quarters ruddy gleams shine out in the distance: an
increasing clamor of smithies is heard around. The clang of
the anvils dies away. A subterranean cavern, stretching farther
than the eye can reach, is now visible, on all sides opening on
to narrow passages.*)

Nibelhome

(Alberich enters, dragging the shrieking Mime from a cleft)

ALBERICH.

He-he! He-he!
Come here! Come here!
Rascally dwarf!
Think of the nips
coming your way,
should you not hurry,
as I command,
to forge the delicate work!

MIME.
(howling)

Ohe! Ohe!
Oh! Oh!
Let me alone!
All's been done
just as you asked.
My toil and sweat
molded the work.
Take out your nails from my ear.

ALBERICH.

Then why the delay
to show it me?

MIME.

I feared that something
you wished was lacking.

ALBERICH.

Why was it not ready?

MIME.
(hesitating)

Here and there.

ALBERICH.

How "here and there"?
Hand me the work.

*(He threatens Mime's ear again. The latter,
terrified, lets fall a piece of metalwork. Alberich picks it up and examines it.)*

Look, you scamp!
All has been fitted
and carefully forged,
just as I wished.
A plague on the rogue!
Would he deceive me
to keep the beautiful
work for himself,
work that my cunning
had taught him?
Do I not know you, thief?

*(He sets the metalwork on his head as a
"Tarnhelm.")*

The helm fits to the head,
but will its magic prove good?
(very softly)

Night and darkness,
hide from me now!

*(His form disappears, replaced by a column
of vapor.)*

See me, O brother?

MIME.
(looking around, astonished)

Where are you? I see you no more.

ALBERICH.
(*invisible*)

Then feel me instead,
you wicked scamp!
(*Mime writhes under blows from an invisible
scourge.*)
Take that for your thievish greed!

MIME.

Ohe! Ohe!
Oh! Oh! Oh!

ALBERICH.

Ha ha ha ha ha ha!
I thank you, numbskull,
your work is tried and true!
Ho ho! Ho ho!
Nibelung elves,
bow down to Alberich!
Now he is everywhere,
watching and spying.
Peace and rest
now have been banished.
Work for your master,
who watches unseen,
and when least you're aware
sees all of your actions.
You're his slaves,
now and forever.
Ho ho! Ho ho!
Hear him, he comes:
the Nibelung lord!
(*The column of vapor disappears. Alberich's
scoldings retreat in the distance. Mime has
cowered down in pain. Wotan and Loge
descend from above by a shaft.*)

LOGE.

Nibelhome's here.
The glare is seen
through the darkness in fiery vapors.

MIME.

Oh! Oh! Oh!

WOTAN.

> Who groans so loud?
> What lies on the stones?

LOGE.
(bending over Mime)

> What marvel's whimpering here?

MIME.

> Ohe! Ohe! Oh! Oh!

LOGE.

> Hey, Mime! Merry dwarf!
> What beats and teases you thus?

MIME.

> Leave me in quiet!

LOGE.

> That will I gladly,
> and more yet, hear!
> Help is coming now, Mime.
> > *(He sets him carefully on his feet.)*

MIME.

> But help from whom?
> I have for master
> the truest of brothers,
> who's bound me fast through his might.

LOGE.

> But Mime, what gave him
> the might of command?

MIME.

> With wicked craft
> Alberich made
> a magic ring
> from gold from the river Rhine.
> At its magic spell
> we tremble, astonished.
> He thus puts in his power
> the Nibelung gnomes of might.
> Once, in our carefree,
> smithing days
> we made gear
> for our women,
> winsomely forged,

delicate Nibelung toys.
We laughed with joy as we toiled.
This wretch now compels us
to slip into chasms.
We're always toiling
only for him.
Through the ring of gold,
he sees in his greed
where shining ore
has been hid in the pits.
And then we must seek it,
find it and dig it,
then smelt the booty,
and forge it to shapes.
With no peace nor pause
we heap the hoard for our lord.

LOGE.

Your idleness may have
roused him to wrath.

MIME.

I'm wretched, ah!
He treats me most cruelly,
I did as told,
forged him a helmet.
He told me in detail
how I should make it.
I shrewdly sensed
the mighty power
instinct in that work,
which I wove of ore.
I wished to keep
the helm for myself,
and with its magic
whisk away Alberich's power.
Perhaps—yes—perhaps
I even might outwit the bully,
subduing his might to my power,
and then with the ring ravished,
I, who had once been the bondsman,
as freeman thence should command!

LOGE.

Then why, my plotter,
had you not luck?

MIME.

Ah, though I forged the wonder,
the magic that gave him joy,
that magic I read not aright.
He who planned my work
then stole my work!
And now to my grief
I found out too late
of the charm hid in the helm.
While I looked he vanished!
But though I was blind,
the blows he gave me were seen!
(*howling and sobbing*)
And such is the thanks
this fool has won!

LOGE.
(*to Wotan*)

Admit, it's not
an easy job.

WOTAN.

Yet the foes will fall,
thanks to your art.
(*Mime observes the gods more attentively.*)
But who are you, strangers,
that ask me these questions?

LOGE.

Friends of yours.
We wish to free
the Nibelung folk from their woe.
(*Hearing Alberich approach, Mime crouches
down.*)

MIME.

Keep a sharp look,
Alberich comes.
(*He runs hither and yon in terror.*)

WOTAN.
(*seating himself on a stone*)
We'll wait your lord here.

*(Alberich, who has taken off the Tarnhelm
and hung it in his girdle, drives with brand-
ished scourge from the caves below a crowd
of Nibelungs before him. They are laden with
gold and silver jewelry, which, under Alberich's continued urging, they pile up to form
a hoard.)*

ALBERICH.

Hither, thither!
He-he! Ho-ho!
Lazy gang!
There in heaps
pile up the hoard!
You there, get up!
Will you move on?
Scandalous folk!
Off with the treasure!
Need any help there?
All of it here!
    (He suddenly perceives Wotan and Loge.)
Hey! Who is there?
Intruders here?
Mime, come here,
scabby old scamp!
Babbling like this
with a vagabond pair!
Off, you no-good!
Off to your forging and welding!
*(He drives Mime with blows of his scourge
            into the gang of Nibelungs.)*
Hey, get to work now!
Off with you! Hurry!
All of you, get!
From those new-found shafts
go dig out the gold!
If any be idle,
Mime shall answer.
He'll find it is hard
to escape a whipping!
That I lurk and watch everywhere,

viewless to all,
I fancy Mime knows well!
Loitering still,
just to waste time?
*(Draws the ring from his finger, kisses it and
                    holds it out threateningly.)*
Fearfully tremble,
you pack of slaves!
Haste for him
who rules the ring.
*(Howls and shrieks as the Nibelungs separate
—Mime among them—and slip back into their
shafts. Alberich watches Wotan and Loge
                    long and mistrustfully.)*

ALBERICH.

Just what do you want?

WOTAN.

We lately heard novel tales
of Nibelhome's mighty land,
dazzling wonders
done here by Alberich,
and eagerness brought us here
to see for ourselves.

ALBERICH.

Your envy
drives you to this place.
I think I know that well,
daring guests.

LOGE.

Since I am known,
simpleton elf,
then say who am I
that you should snarl!
You shivered once
within a cold hole.
Where were your light
and comforting fire
if Loge had not been there,
and where were your forging
had I not heated the forge?
Though I'm your cousin

and was your friend,
I don't think much of your thanks!

ALBERICH.

You smile now,
on light-elves, Loge,
you cunning rogue!
Are you, false one, their friend,
as you once were my own?
Ha ha! That's fine,
I need not fear them at all.

LOGE.

I think I'm worthy your trust.

ALBERICH.

I can trust your untruth but not
    your truth!
I'm secure,
and I defy you!

LOGE.

It's your might
has made you so bold.
Grimly great
waxes your strength!

ALBERICH.

Look at the hoard
which my host piled in a heap.

LOGE.

I never have seen one so fine.

ALBERICH.

That's for today
the merest trifle!
Bravely towering it will grow in the
    future!

WOTAN.

But what's your use for the hoard
in joyless Nibelhome
where nothing's bought with such wealth?

ALBERICH.

Treasures to garner
and treasures to bury,
so serves Nibelhome's might.

But with the hoard
that is heaped high in caves
watch for the wonder I'm planning:
the gold I gain
will win me rule of this planet.

WOTAN.

How, my good man, can you do that?

ALBERICH.

You who, lapped in balmy airs,
up there above live,
laugh and love:
my golden grip
shall totter you gods to your downfall!
As I have forsworn love for good,
all things that live,
too, shall forswear it!
Ensnared by my gold,
just gold alone shall you long for!
On glorious heights,
in exquisite raptures
rock yourselves!
The elves meet your scorn,
you reveling immortals!
Take care!
take care!
For when you men
first serve my commands,
then your proud-decked women
with their scorn for my love
shall serve my pleasure at will,
though love shall be out!

(laughing wildly)

Ha ha ha ha!
Have I been heard?
Beware!
Beware of the armies of night,
when the Nibelung hoard shall arise
from silent darkness—to day!

WOTAN.
(starting)

Away, rascally wretch!

ALBERICH.

What says he?

LOGE.

Back to your senses!
Who can keep back his wonder
when seeing Alberich's work?
If what you have planned with the hoard
prospers through masterly cunning,
I surely must hail you as mightiest;
for moon and stars,
and the sun in his glory,
even they must accept you—
also serve you as thralls.
Yet, let me warn you to keep
all of your Nibelung heapers
of gold in a state
free from servile hate.
You have deft touch of your ring:
your people tremble with fear.
Yet if a thief
slipped in while you slept,
and then pulled off your ring,
what, wise one, would come of your
plans?

ALBERICH.

He thinks himself sharp and clever,
but he deems
all others are fools!
He hopes I am needing
aid and advice—
on iron terms.
The thief would enjoy the thought!
The helmet that hides
was planned by myself.
The cunningest smith,
Mime, forged it to order.
Fast it transforms me

just as I wish
to a form that is different.
Thus the helm.
No one sees me,
much as he tries.
Yet, though I am hidden,
I still can perform.
I am free from care,
and safe even from you,
my fine, provident friend!

LOGE.

Much I've looked at,
some of it wondrous,
but have not witnessed
a thing like this.
This work without equal
sounds like a fable.
If this can really happen,
then your might's truly quite boundless!

ALBERICH.

Think you I lie
and prattle like Loge?

LOGE.

Till it is proved,
friend dwarf, I doubt your word.

ALBERICH.

Your cunning, blockhead,
has filled you to bursting.
Now, plague on your spite.
Decide right here on the shape
you would like me to take.

LOGE.

Whatever you will,
but make me mute with amaze!

ALBERICH.
(*putting on the Tarnhelm*)
"Giant snake,
coiling and winding!"

*(He instantly disappears and in his place
writhes a monstrous serpent on the ground.
It rears and opens its outstretched jaws at
Wotan and Loge.)*

LOGE.
(pretending fear)

Ohe! Ohe!

WOTAN.
(laughing)

Ha ha ha! Ha ha ha!
Good, Alberich!

LOGE.

Horrible serpent,
don't swallow me up!
Spare the life of poor Loge!

WOTAN.

Good, you rascal!
How fast the dwarf
has grown to a dragonish foe!
*(The serpent disappears and Alberich reap-
pears in his natural form.)*

ALBERICH.

Ha ha! you smart ones!
Now do you know?

LOGE.
(his voice quavering)

My trembling, surely, should prove it!
You made the monstrous
serpent with speed!
Now that I've seen,
I confess to the wonder.
Since you grew greater,
can you grow smaller
and be quite tiny?
The smartest way, I think,
to hide from dangerous foes.
But maybe that is too hard.

ALBERICH.

Too hard? Yes,
if you are dumb!

How small shall I be?

LOGE.

That the smallest crack may contain you—
a size just right for a toad.

ALBERICH.

Pah! Quite easy! Look at me now!
(He puts on the helmet.)
"Creeping toad,
gray and crooked!"
*(He vanishes, and a toad is seen crawling on
the rocks.)*

LOGE.
(to Wotan)

There! He did it!
Capture him, quick!
*(Wotan sets his foot on the toad. Loge puts
his hand to its head and seizes the Tarnhelm.)*

ALBERICH.

Oho! Accurst!
Now they have caught me!

LOGE.

Hold him fast,
till he is bound!
*(Alberich suddenly becomes visible in his
own shape, writhing under Wotan's foot.)*

LOGE.
(binding him with bast rope)

Up we go fast!
There we shall hold him!

*(The prisoner, though trying furiously to escape, is dragged
by both to the shaft from which they descended. There they
disappear, mounting upward. The scene now changes again,
but in the reverse direction. Anvils are heard until we reach
the upper regions. There Wotan and Loge, with the pinioned
Alberich mount from the cleft.)*

An Open Space on the Mountain Heights

(A pale mist shrouds all.)

LOGE.

There, kinsman,
take a seat here!
Look, beloved,
there lies the world
which the lazybones wishes to rule.
What corner, pray,
is set aside for my stall?
(He dances around him, snapping his fingers.)

ALBERICH.

Scandalous schemer!
You rogue! You thief!
Loosen the rope!
Get me untied!
Or, villain, you'll surely regret it!

WOTAN.

You're really caught now,
fast in my fetters,
just when you dreamed
that all that lived
were ready to be your servants.
You lie now, bound at my feet.
You cannot, trembler, deny it.
To let you go free
we must have a ransom.

ALBERICH.

I'm a dolt,
a fool in a dream
to have faith
in such treacherous tricks!
Fearful revenge
shall pay for my fault!

LOGE.

For vengeance to help you,
you first must talk yourself free!
To a fettered man
no free man answers for outrage.
So, since you want vengeance,
swift, that delays not,
think of the ransom we ask.
(*He snaps his fingers, indicating the kind of
ransom.*)

ALBERICH.

Then state, what are your terms?

WOTAN.

The hoard and your gleaming gold.

ALBERICH.

Greedy and criminal crew!

(*aside*)

If I still have the magic ring
I freely may give them the hoard,
for I soon will be able to build one anew,
through the magical might of the ring.
Here's a lesson, I think,
that sharpens my wit.
I think I'm getting off cheap,
losing a toy and nothing else.

WOTAN.

Now what of the hoard?

ALBERICH.

Loosen my hand,
I'll have it brought in.
(*Loge unties his right hand. Alberich puts the
ring to his lips and murmurs a secret spell.*)
All right! The Nibelungs

will come at my call!
They obey my orders.
Mark how they march
from the depths to the day with the hoard.
Now loosen these burdensome bonds!

WOTAN.

No use, till all has been paid.

(The Nibelungs ascend from the cleft, laden with the treasures of the hoard, which they start to pile up.)

ALBERICH.

O, shameful disgrace,
that my timid varlets
should view me shackled like this.

(to the Nibelungs)

Carry it there
as I command!
Make a pile!
Heap it up high!
Need any help there?
But don't look this way!
Quick there! Quick!
Then hurry and leave us!
Off to your jobs!
Back to your mine pits!
Woe to laggards at work!
I shall follow close at your heels!

(He kisses his ring and stretches it out commandingly. As if struck by a blow the Nibelungs rush in fear and terror to the cleft, into which they slip.)

I've paid fully,
now let me leave.
And the smithied helm
that Loge has there,
be good now and give it back!

LOGE.
(throwing the Tarnhelm upon the hoard)

We take it as part of the booty.

ALBERICH.

> Accursed thief!
> Yet wait a while!
> He who forged me the first,
> let him repeat it.
> I still hold the might
> that Mime obeys.
> Bad indeed
> to yield my foes
> weapons I need for defense!
> Now then, everything
> has been given.
> Now loose—you bad men—my bonds.

LOGE.

> Are you contented?
> Should he be freed?

WOTAN.

> A golden ring
> shows on your finger.
> Hear me, elf.
> That also belongs with the hoard.
> To get your freedom,
> that must be left us.

ALBERICH.
(stunned)

> The ring?
> My life then, but not the ring.

WOTAN.
(more violently)

> I ask the ring too:
> with your life just do as you please.

ALBERICH.

> But if my life is left me,
> the ring too must be included.
> Hand and head,
> eye and ear—
> they are mine no more
> than this ring that is called my own.

WOTAN.

> You really call it your own?

Shameless elf, are you not raving?
Simply say
where you borrowed the gold
from which you have welded the ring.
Did you own it
when you took it
from out the depths of the Rhine?
Ask the river maidens
whether they said
that they gave you
their gold for possession
which you have robbed for your ring!

ALBERICH.

Shameful malignance!
Scandalous fraud!
Would you, villainy,
blame me for the deed
you dreamt of yourself?
Yourself you would have
gladly stolen the gold,
had it been
just as easy to forge as to steal.
You hypocrite,
how lucky you are
that the Nibelung here,
in shameful despite,
in a wave of wrath,
won the gold with its terrible charm,
whose work now smiles on you fair.
The unhallowed one's
anguish-ridden,
curse-harboring,
terrible deed,
is only a toy
for a prince's amusement.
Shall peace be your prize for my curse?
Guard yourself,
conquering god!
When I do sin.

I sin to myself alone.
But the virtuous god
sins against all
that was, is and will be,
if rashly he seizes my ring!

WOTAN.

Yield the ring!
What good is babbling
to prove you are right.
(*He seizes Alberich and tears the ring from
his fingers.*)

ALBERICH.
(*shrieking horribly*)

I'm shattered
and crushed,
the saddest of sorrowful slaves!

WOTAN.
(*contemplating the ring*)

I hold here what sets me up—
the strongest of mightiest lords!
(*He puts the ring on.*)

LOGE.
(*to Wotan*)

Is he released?

WOTAN.

Set him free!
(*Loge completely unties Alberich's bonds.*)

LOGE.
(*to Alberich*)

Slip away home!
No more fetters bind you!
Fare freely from here!

ALBERICH.
(*raising himself*)

Am I now free?
(*with a raging laugh*)

Really free?
I greet you then
with my freedom's first salute!
As the ring came as a curse,
so cursed be it now!

Through its gold
came measureless might,
now let its lords
find measureless death.
Let none rejoice,
owning the ring.
Let no gleam from it
shine on a happy mind!
Care shall consume
the ones who possess it,
and envy gnaw those
who wish that they did!
Each shall lust
after its delights,
yet no one shall find
any profit there!
Let its owner never be blest,
Let it draw the slayer to his doom!
Let death be his portion,
fear be the bread that he eats!
And while he lives,
let him long for his death—
this treasure's lord
as the treasure's slave,
till I hold again
in my hand the ring I was robbed of!
Thus, urged by
the sorest of spite,
the Nibelung blesses his ring.
So keep it now,

(laughing)

guard it with care!

(wrathfully)

But you can't flee from my curse!
*(He disappears into the cleft. The thick vapor
gradually clears off.)*

LOGE.

Did you mark
all his words of love?

WOTAN.
(absorbed in contemplation of the ring)
>Grant him the joy of complaint!
>>*(It continues to get lighter.)*

LOGE.
(looking into the distance)
>Fasolt and Fafner soon will be here.
>Freia follows them here.
>>*(Out of the still dispersing mist emerge Donner, Froh and Fricka.)*

FROH.
>They're on their way back!

DONNER.
>You're welcome, brother!

FRICKA.
(anxiously to Wotan)
>Have you brought good tidings?

LOGE.
(pointing to the hoard)
>With cunning and force
>we did the work.
>Right there lies Freia's price.

DONNER.
>See the fair one come,
>free of the giants.

FROH.
>How lovely the air
>wafting again!
>Feelings of joy
>are filling our thoughts!
>Think of how we would suffer,
>forever parted from her
>who lends us life without sorrow,
>youth that is endless in joy.
>>*(Fasolt and Fafner enter, leading Freia between them. Fricka hastens joyfully toward her sister. The gods appear restored in aspect. In the background, however, there still hovers a veil of mist, keeping the distant castle invisible.)*

FRICKA.

Loveliest sister!
Sweetest delight!
Have you returned as our ransom?

FASOLT.
(*stopping her*)

Halt! Hold off a while!
Freia still is ours.
We rested some,
there on the ridge,
Gianthome's mark.
We took best care
of our bargain's pledge,
treating her fair,
I've brought her back,
but much regret this.
Now pay us brothers
the ransom due.

WOTAN.

Right there lies the ransom.
The golden mass
must be fittingly measured.

FASOLT.

To lose this maiden
really will sadden my heart.
But there's a way to forget her:
pile the treasure hoard
high in a heap,
so as to cover
all of the fair one from me.

WOTAN.

Then place the girl
as gauge for the heap!

(*The two giants set Freia in the middle. Then they thrust their staves into the ground on each side of her, so as to measure her height and breadth.*)

FAFNER.

Our staves have been planted

to gauge her form.
Now heap the hoard to this height.

WOTAN.

Haste with the work.
Really distasteful!

LOGE.

Help me, Froh!

FROH.

I must end
Freia's dishonor.
*(Loge and Froh heap up the treasure between
the staves.)*

FAFNER.

Not so light
and loose with this heap!
*(He roughly presses the ornaments closer to-
gether.)*
Tight and close, fill up the gauge!
(He looks for crevices.)
I still can see through,
so fill in the openings!

LOGE.

Get back, you lubber!

FAFNER.

Come here!

LOGE.

Leave it alone!

FAFNER.

Come here!
This chink must be closed!

WOTAN.
(turning away, downcast)
Deep is the shame
burning my breast!

FRICKA.

Deep is the shame,
there where the fair one stands!
And she hopes for help,
mute, with sorrowful gaze!
Wicked man!
It's you brought our dear one to this!

FAFNER.

Still more! Still more this way!

DONNER.

This is too much!
Shameless, this rogue
wakens my ravening rage.
Come here, you dog!
Must you measure,
then match yourself against me!

FAFNER.

Calmly, Donner!
Not so much noise!
We need no rumblings from you.

DONNER.
(aiming a blow)

Not to shake you to pieces?

WOTAN.

Be at peace!
I think she's covered by now.

LOGE.
(watching Fafner measure the hoard critically)

The hoard gives out!

FAFNER.

The sheen of her hair still shows.
Toss on that trinket
with the rest.

LOGE.

What? Even the helm?

FAFNER.

Quickly! Here with it!

WOTAN.

Let it go also!
(Loge throws it on the heap.)

LOGE.

So now we are ready!
Anything further?

FASOLT.

Freia, the radiant,
passes from sight.

I see she's redeemed.
Must I now leave her?

(He goes up to the hoard and peeps through
it.)

Ah! Her glance
yet gleams on me here.
Her starry eyes
dazzle my own.
I still can spy them
right through this space.

(excited)

And I can't part from this woman
while I see the grace of one eye.

FAFNER.

Ha! I warn you
to stop up that cranny!

LOGE.

Never sated!
Can you not see
our hoard is all spent!

FAFNER.

Not wholly, friend!
On Wotan's finger
gleams a ring made of gold.
Give that to fill up the cranny.

WOTAN.

What! Give the ring?

LOGE.

Let me tell you,
the Rhine-daughters
must have this gold.
Wotan plans soon to restore it.

WOTAN.

What babbling is this?
I sweated for this booty!
I shall keep it fearlessly mine!

LOGE.

That means ruin
to the promise
I gave the sorrowing maids!

WOTAN.

What you said's not binding to me.
The ring is booty I won.

FAFNER.

Now add the final
part of the ransom.

WOTAN.

Ask as much as you will,
all will be granted;
but all the world
cannot make me give up the ring.
*(Fasolt angrily pulls Freia from behind the
hoard.)*

FASOLT.

All is off!
The old way stands.
We'll keep your Freia forever!

FREIA.

Help me! Help me!

FRICKA.

Haughty god!
Do as they ask!

FROH.

Hold not the gold back!

DONNER.

Give them the ring too!
*(Fafner holds back Fasolt, who is hurrying
away.)*

WOTAN.

Leave me alone!
The ring stays with me!
(He turns away in wrath.)
*(The scene darkens. From the rocky cleft at
the side breaks forth a bluish light, in which
Erda suddenly becomes visible, rising up to
half her height from below. She stretches out
a warning hand to Wotan.)*

ERDA.

Yield it, Wotan! Yield it!
Flee the cursed ring!

Dark and despairing destruction
marks its owner's end!

WOTAN.

Who are you, woman of doom?

ERDA.

Great is my lore. Hearken!
All things that were,
all things that happen,
all to be,
are known to me.
Prime-Vala,
Erda, bids you beware.
Three the daughters
born to me
long before earth was.
What I witness,
nightly the Norns tell to Wotan.
But direst of danger
has brought me
to your aid.
Hear me! Hear me! Hear me!
All things that are, perish!
A mournful day
dawns for Valhalla.
I warn you, give up the ring!
*(Erda sinks into the earth to her breast, while
the bluish glow begins to fade.)*

WOTAN.

A lofty lore
sounds in your words.
Wait! Let me hear more wisdom!

ERDA.
(sinking)

I've warned you well.
You know enough.
Weigh and fear my words!
*(She disappears completely. Wotan seeks to
follow and stop her. Froh and Fricka throw
themselves in his way and hold him back.)*

WOTAN.

> Why this fear and this worry!
> I must detain you,
> so I'll know all things!

FRICKA.

> What would you, maniac?

FROH.

> Take care, Wotan!
> Fear what she tells you!
> Hark to her words!
> *(Wotan gazes thoughtfully before him.)*

DONNER.
(turning to the giants resolutely)

> Hear, you giants!
> Go back! Just wait there!
> The gold, Wotan will give you.

FREIA.

> Dare I to hope it!
> Well, is Holda
> worthy the price required?
> *(All look expectantly toward Wotan. He, rousing himself from deep thought, grasps his spear and brandishes it.)*

WOTAN.

> Then stay, Freia!
> I set you free.
> Bought back again,
> now let our youth be restored!
> You giants, here is your ring!
> *(He throws the ring upon the hoard. The giants release Freia. She hastens joyfully to the gods, who embrace her in turn, for some time, with the greatest delight.)*
>
> *(Fafner has meanwhile spread out a huge sack, and busies himself over the hoard, preparing to pack it in.)*

FASOLT.
(to Fafner)

> Stop, you greedy rogue!
> Give me some also!

Fairly and squarely
both should share it.

FAFNER.

Amorous dolt, you prefer
gold to the girl, I see.
I found it hard
to make you exchange it,
when in desire
to woo her
you thought not to share.
Therefore shall I
keep for my portion
the greatest part of the hoard.

FASOLT.

Treacherous thief!
Insolent rogue!

(to the gods)

Come, give us your judgment!
See that we fairly
share in the hoard!
(Wotan turns contemptuously away.)

LOGE.

Let him take the treasure.
*(Fasolt throws himself on Fafner, who is
busily packing up.)*
Keep for yourself just the ring!

FASOLT.

Away! You cheater! Mine is the ring!
I bought it with Freia's glance!
*(He snatches hastily at the ring. They strug-
gle. Fasolt wrests the ring from Fafner.)*

FAFNER.

Off with your fist!
The ring is mine!

FASOLT.

I hold it, for I own it!

FAFNER.
(hitting out with his staff)
Hold it tight or it may fall!
*(With one stroke he fells Fasolt, then wrests
the ring from his dying grasp.)*

Now blink upon Freia's face!
You shall no more touch the ring!
(He puts it into the sack and then resumes his
packing.)

WOTAN.
(horrified)

Fearful force
resides in the mighty curse!

LOGE.

What luck, Wotan,
happens as your luck?
What you won
was a great achievement.
Now it's taken away though—
that's better yet!
For your foemen, see,
having your gold,
bring about their doom themselves.

WOTAN.

Yet a horror enchains me.
Care and fear
fetter my soul.
Erda shall teach me
how I may end it.
I must go to her now!

FRICKA.
(approaching him cajolingly)

Why tarry, then, Wotan?
See how your noble
castle gleams,
gladly awaiting
Wotan, lord of its life.

WOTAN.
(gloomily)

A dreadful price
paid for that hall!

DONNER.
(pointing toward the back, which is still veiled in mist)

Sweltering mist
hangs in the air.

Thick the pressure
of turbid air.
I'll gather the clouds,
bringing the lightning and thunder,
and clear the fog from the sky!
*(Donner mounts a high rock by the precipice
and there swings his hammer. During the
following the mists collect round him.)*
He da! He da! He do!
Come hither, you dews!
Come hither, you mists!
Donner, your lord,
calls you to arms!

(He swings his hammer.)
As this hammer swings,
marshal your ranks!
Vaporly damps!
Hovering dews!
Donner, your lord,
calls you to arms!
He da! He da! He do!
*(Donner completely disappears in an ever-
thickening and darkening thundercloud. His
hammer-stroke is heard to fall heavily on the
rocks. A vivid lightning flash darts through
the cloud. A violent thunderclap follows.
Froh has also disappeared in the clouds.)*

DONNER.
(invisible)

Brother, come here!
Show us the way to the bridge!
*(Suddenly the clouds disperse. Donner and
Froh become visible. From their feet stretches
in blinding radiance a rainbow-bridge over
the valley to the castle, which now gleams in
the light of the setting sun.)*

FROH.
*(pointing to the bridge with his outstretched hand, as the way
over the valley.)*
This bridge to the castle
light, yet firm underfoot,

may now be trod
with a step free of fear!
*(Wotan and the other gods are speechless
    with astonishment at the glorious sight.)*

WOTAN.

As it sets,
sun's bright eye is glowing.
Its glorious gleam
gilds tower and wall.
In the radiant dawn
it shimmered so bravely,
lying masterless,
nobly greeting its lord.
From morning till evening,
through toil and care,
and not through joy, grew its portals.
The night is nigh.
Against its spite,
friendly our shelter looms.
So, hail to our home,
refuge from fear and dread!
                    (He turns solemnly to Fricka.)
Follow me, wife!
Let Valhall harbor us both.

FRICKA.

Just what is this Valhall!
I've never heard you once name it!

WOTAN.

The fort I have found
to finish all fear,
if born to success,
soon will explain its name.

*(He grasps Fricka by the hand and paces
with her slowly toward the bridge. Froh,
                    Freia and Donner follow.)*

LOGE.
(remaining behind)

Now behold them haste to their end,
while they fancy their being immortal!
I feel ashamed

to share in their actions.
A burning temptation
to flare into blazes
builds a wish in my heart
to burn those up
who had once made me tame,
rather than blindly
die with the blind—
although they are gods the most godlike!
I think that is the thing!
I'll give it some thought.
Who knows what I'll do?
*(He goes up with assumed carelessness to join
the gods. The three Rhine maidens are heard
below in the valley, invisible.)*

RHINE MAIDS.

Rhinegold! Rhinegold!
Purest gold!
How brightly you glowed,
shining so fair on us!
For you, our radiance,
we are mourning.
Give us our gold!
O, give us our radiance again!

LOGE.
(looking down in to the valley)
The Rhine-king's children
mourn for their stolen gold!

WOTAN.
(who has paused at the bridge)
What mourning rings in my ears!
Accursed nixies!
Stop their harrowing noise!

LOGE.
(calling down into the valley)
You in the water!
just why do you wail?
Hear what Wotan desires:
nevermore

seek the gleam of the gold!
And instead enjoy the brave new gleam
that comes from the gods!
*(The gods laugh and during the following
cross the bridge.)*

RHINE MAIDS.

Rhinegold!
Rhinegold!
Rarest gold!
O may our bright toy
shine again
in the depths of Rhine!
What's in the deep
holds truth and uprightness!
False and weak
is what rejoices above!

THE END

THE VALKYRIE

CHARACTERS

SIEGMUND, *the Volsung*

HUNDING

WOTAN, *King of the Gods*

SIEGLINDA, *Siegmund's Sister*

BRUNNHILDA, *the Valkyrie*

FRICKA, *the Goddess of Wedlock*

VALKYRIE MAIDENS: *Gerhilda, Ortlinda, Valtrauta, Schwertleita, Helmviga, Siegruna, Grimgerda, Rossveissa*

THE VALKYRIE

ACT ONE

The Interior of a Dwelling

In the center is the stem of a mighty ash tree, whose roots spread far over the ground. The tree is separated from its crown by a timber roof which is pierced to allow the spreading limbs to pass through. Round the trunk a room is built; the walls are of roughly-hewn logs, hung here and there with matting and woven hangings. To the right, in the foreground, is the fireplace, behind which is an inner room like a storeroom, approached by mounting a few steps, and separated from the forepart of the hall by a plaited curtain, half thrown back. In the background an entrance door with a wooden latch. Farther in the front, but on the same side, there is a table, and behind it a broad wooden bench fastened to the wall; a few wooden stools stand before the table.

After a brief orchestral prelude of a wild and stormy character, Siegmund hastily opens the entrance door from without and enters. It is nearly evening; a violent thunderstorm is just subsiding. Siegmund holds the latch in his hand for a moment and scans the room. He looks exhausted, and his disordered garments indicate a fugitive. Perceiving no one he closes the door behind him, strides to the hearth and there throws himself down, exhausted, on a rug of bearskin.

SIEGMUND.

No matter whose hearth,
here I must slumber.
(*He sinks back and remains stretched out
motionless a while. Sieglinda enters through
the door of the inner chamber. She is a little
astonished.*)

SIEGLINDA.

A stranger here!
I must accost him.
(*She advances a few steps.*)
Who is this man
that lies by the hearth?
(*As he does not stir, she approaches still
nearer and observes him.*)
Really weary
and travel-worn!
Maybe unconscious too!
Could he be sick?
(*She bends closer to him.*)
His breath is still coming;
his eyes remain closed, though.
Brave and strong seems the man,
though he fell fatigued.

SIEGMUND.
(*suddenly lifting his head*)
A drink! A drink!

SIEGLINDA.

I'll fetch one for you.
(*She quickly takes a drinking horn, leaves
the house, returns with the horn filled, which
she hands to Siegmund.*)
Here's refreshment
for lips that are parching:
water, which you did want.
(*Siegmund drinks and returns the horn. After
a nod of thanks he regards her with increasing attention.*)

SIEGMUND.

Cooling refreshment

came from the spring:
my weight of woe
now is more light.
My courage returns.
My eye enjoys
the blessed pleasure of sight—
But who restores me to life?

SIEGLINDA.

This house and this wife
belong to Hunding.
Let him welcome his guest:
stay till he comes back home!

SIEGMUND.

Weaponless am I.
The wounded guest
cannot worry your husband.

SIEGLINDA.

Oh, show your wounds right away!

SIEGMUND.
(Shakes himself and springs up quickly to a sitting position.)
They're scratches, all.
There's nothing to see.
My limbs are still firmly
fixed in their frame.
Had my shield and spear been as good,
half as strong as my arm was,
never would I have fled.
But my spear and my shield are gone.
The hounds oppressed and
harried me hard,
and raging storms
spent all my strength.
Yet fast as I fled the hunters,
faster weariness went.
Night fell, with a rest to my eyes.
the sun now smiles in my face.

SIEGLINDA.
(Has filled a horn with mead, and extends it to him.)
I trust you will take this

mellow mead,
sweet in its creamy taste.

SIEGMUND.

Will you not taste it first?
*(Sieglinda does so, then hands him the horn
again. Siegmund takes a long draught, then
returns the horn. For a long time the two
remain silent, looking at each other with
growing interest.)*
You have helped one who is Fortune's foe.
May all evil
be turned from you.
     (He rises hastily, as if about to leave.)
I've rested sweetly,
and feel refreshed.
Now I'll go on my way.

SIEGLINDA.

Who pursues you, that you must flee?

SIEGMUND.

Misfortune hunts me
in all my fleeings.
Misfortune dogs me
in all my goings.
May all this keep from you far!
Now must I take my leave.
     (He goes to the door, and lifts the latch.)

SIEGLINDA.

Stay here instead!
You bring no sorrow within,
where sorrow already dwells.

SIEGMUND.
*(Deeply moved, remains motionless and searches Sieglinda's
features. Finally he returns, and resumes his seat by the hearth.)*
Woe-king—that is my name,
so I'll wait here for Hunding.
*(Sieglinda remains in silence; then she starts,
and listens. Hunding is heard leading his
horse to the stable outside. She hastens to
open the door. Hunding enters, armed with
shield and spear. In the doorway he stops on
beholding Siegmund.)*

SIEGLINDA.
(meeting her husband's questioning look)
> Here he fell,
> weary and worn.
> Need brought him inside.

HUNDING.
> You tended him?

SIEGLINDA.
> I cooled his thirsty lips
> as a hostess should.

SIEGMUND.
> Food and drink,
> thanks to her.
> Then will you call her guilty?

HUNDING.
> Holy is my hearth,
> holy to you my house.
>> *(to Sieglinda, giving her his weapons)*
> Bring the food for us men.
> *(Sieglinda hangs the weapons on the tree,
> fetches food and drink from the storeroom
> and sets the table.)*

HUNDING.
*(scanning Siegmund's features sharply and comparing them
with those of his wife)*
> How strong the resemblance!
> Through eyes like to hers
> gleams the glittering serpent.
>> *(He turns with apparent unconcern to Sieg-
>> mund.)*
> Far indeed
> must you have fared!
> You rode no steed,
> yet found this place.
> What sorry pathway
> led to your woe?

SIEGMUND.
> Through wood and meadow,
> thicket and heath,
> storm drove me forth,
> and pressing need.

I know not the way that I came.
Nor do I better
know where I've come to.
This is now what I would learn.

HUNDING.
(at the table, and beckoning Siegmund to a seat)
The roof above,
the house around—
these are Hunding's own.
If you go west
when you leave this place
you'll reach my kin
in their rich homesteads.
They guard the honor of Hunding.
May I ask of my guest
to inform me now of his name?
*(Siegmund remains thoughtfully silent. Sieg-
linda, seated beside Hunding, opposite Siegmund, fixes her eyes on the latter.)*

HUNDING.

Should you fear to
show me your trust,
my wife here likes to listen.
See, she hangs upon your words!

SIEGLINDA.

Guest, I would learn
who you are.

SIEGMUND.

"Peaceful" no one should name me;
"Joyful"—would that I were!
Just let me call myself "Woe-king"!
Wolfe—he was my father.
I came one of a pair.
We were twins, my sister and I.
Both did I lose,
mother and maid,
she who gave birth,
and my partner in birth.
Short was the time they were mine.
Wolfe was strong and stalwart,

but foes were many and fierce.
The father fared
to the hunt with the youngster.
One time we returned
all tired from the hunt,
and found our lair laid waste.
Our lordly hall
was ruined by fire,
our oak once blooming,
now was a stump.
My mother lay murdered,
brave-hearted soul!
All trace of my sister
was lost in wrack.
The Neidings' cruel band
were cause of this bitter deed.
My father fled,
an outcast with me.
Years and years the
youngster did live with
his father within the wild.
Many hunts
were made for the two,
but still the wolf-pair
withstood their foes.

(to Hunding)

A Wolfing tells you of this,
whom as Wolfing many well know.

HUNDING.

Wild and amazing stories
certainly, doughty guest,
Woe-king—the Wolfing!
I think I have heard of this pair,
through dark and evil rumors.
Wolf though, or Wolfing
I've never known.

SIEGLINDA.

But tell me further, stranger,
where dwells your father now?

SIEGMUND.

A mighty outcry was raised.
Neidings were hot on our heels.
But many hunters
fell to the Wolfings,
in flight through the woods
slain by their game!
Our foe was scattered like chaff.
My father, though, vanished just then,
and he left no traces
though long I did seek him.
And a wolfskin was all
that I ever found.
Then my wish, shunning the woods,
now drew me to menfolk and women.
The ones I found,
no matter where,
though friends to know,
or maids to woo,
always gave scorn to the outcast.
Evil lay on me.
Whatever I thought right
others looked on as wrong.
What looked evil to me
others favored as right!
No matter where I went
there was strife.
Wrath found me,
go where I would.
When I sought pleasure
Sorrow was found.
And so I am rightly "Woe-king,"
for sorrow only is mine.

HUNDING.

With so sad a lot as your share,
the Norns are not your friends.
No one greets you with joy
to whom you come as guest.

SIEGLINDA.

Only cowards would fear

a weaponless, lonely man.
Tell me yet, guest,
how in the strife
you lost your weapon at last.

SIEGMUND.
(more animatedly)

A child in distress
called for my help.
Her kinsmen wanted
to marry the maiden
to one whom her heart could not love.
Straightway I went,
eager to aid.
I gave the gang
trouble to spare.
The victor felled the foes.
Struck down in death lay the brothers.
The maiden clung fast to her slain.
Her wrath gave place to her grief.
She poured forth floods of tears.
She wailed the hardness of fate.
At the loss of the slaughtered brothers
loud were the cries of the bride.
Then the slain men's kinsmen
stormed to the place,
overwhelming,
eager to venge themselves.
Foemen came raging,
circling the homestead.
Yet would the maid
cling to her dead.
My spear and shield
guarded her long,
till spear and shield
were hewn from my grip.
Standing weaponless, wounded,
I beheld the bride die,
while warriors were pressing me hard.
On the corpses she lay dead.
(Looking at Sieglinda with pained fervor)

You know now, questioning wife,
why my name cannot be "Peaceful."
(*He gets up and steps over to the hearth.
Sieglinda casts down her eyes, deeply
moved.*)

HUNDING.
(*very darkly*)

I know a riotous race:
it does not revere
what others do.
It's hated by all, and by me.
I heard the summons to vengeance,
payment demanded
for blood of kin.
I came too late,
went back to my home,
and found the cursed tracks
within my very own house.
For now, Wolfing,
you are secure.
For this night you are my guest.
But arm yourself with
strong weapons tomorrow:
that day is chosen for strife.
You'll pay me what the deed pays.
(*to Sieglinda, who has anxiously stepped between the two men.*)

Out of the room!
Loiter not here!
Prepare my drink for the night,
and wait for me within.
(*Pensively, Sieglinda takes a drinking horn
from the table, goes to a cupboard from
which she takes spices, and turns toward the
chamber. On reaching the uppermost step
near the door she again turns her head toward
Siegmund, who stands calmly and sullenly by
the hearth, never losing sight of her. She
casts at him a long and significant glance, by
which she endeavors to direct his attention
to a spot in the ash tree. Hunding, noticing*

*the delay, warns her off with a commanding
look. She disappears through the door with
the torch and drinking horn.)*

HUNDING.

(taking his weapons from the tree)

A man has need of his arms.
I'll see you, Wolfing, with morning.
You heard what I said—
guard yourself well!
(He goes into the chamber with his arms.)
*(Night has fallen. The hall is dimly lit by the
dying fire. Siegmund sinks down on the bench
by the fire, and reflects, with some perturbation.)*

SIEGMUND.

I'd find a sword, said my father,
in time of my greatest need.
Swordless I came here,
my host a foe.
As his vengeance' pledge
here do I stand.
a wife hailed me,
noble and fair.
A lovely anguish
burns my heart.
The woman for whom I long,
she whose magic casts a sweet spell,
is held in thrall by the man
who scorns one who's unarmed.
Volsa, Volsa,
where is your sword,
that mighty sword
I can swing in battle?
Does there now break from my breast
what raged in my heart till now?
*(The fire falls together. From the aroused
glow a bright ray strikes that spot of the ash
tree stem Sieglinda had indicated where a
buried sword hilt is now revealed.)*
What glistens there
in glimmering light?

From the ash stem
I perceive a gleam.
Unseeing eyes are
lit by its look.
See, it laughs in my face.
How my heart takes fire
to see it shine.
Is it the glance
the glorious wife
left behind her
to cling to the tree
as she went out the hall?
(*The fire on the hearth is beginning to die
out.*)

Deepening darkness
shadowed my eyes,
but the glance she shed
brightened my gloom,
bringing me daylight and warmth.
Sweet the sunlight
appeared to me.
It scattered around me
its radiant glance,
till mountains hid it from view.
Yet once more ere it set
came the blessing again.
And the ancient ash's stem
was lit by the golden glow.
The flush has faded.
The light grows dim.
Gathering darkness
weighs on my eyelids.
Deep in my quiet bosom
gleams an invisible flame.
(*The fire has quite gone out. It is deep night.
The chamber door opens softly. Sieglinda in
a white robe enters and approaches Sieg-
mund.*)

SIEGLINDA.

Sleeping, guest?

SIEGMUND.
(springing up with joyful surprise)
> Who steals this way?

SIEGLINDA.

> It's I, listen to me!
> In heavy sleep lies Hunding.
> I mingled a drug with his drink.
> Use up the night to your good!

SIEGMUND.
(interrupting)

> Good comes when you're near!

SIEGLINDA.

> Let me guide you now to a weapon.
> O might you win this sword!
> I then might call you
> noblest of heroes.
> The strongest alone
> bears off the prize.
> O, mark it well, all that I tell you!
> The band of kinsmen
> sat here in hall,
> invited as guests to his wedding.
> He courted a maid
> whom, quite unasked,
> villains had brought him for bride.
> Sad I sat there,
> while they were drinking.
> A stranger entered the hall,
> an old man, suited in gray.
> Pulled down was his hat
> so one of his eyes was hidden.
> Yet the other's glare
> put all in terror.
> All the guests felt
> its threatening force.
> I alone
> felt from its power
> sweet, longing distress,
> comfort and tears combined.
> On me looking,

he scowled at the others,
as he swung a sword in his hands,
then drove it deep
in the ash's stem,
till it went up to the hilt.
There's one who can win the weapon
he who can draw it out.
But all who tried it,
despite all their efforts,
at last were forced to give up.
Guests were coming,
and guests were going,
the strongest tugged at the steel—
But they could not budge it a bit.
The sword is resting there still.
I knew then who it was
that had greeted me in gloom.
I know too
who alone
must pull the sword from the tree.
O, if I could find
today, that friend,
come from afar
who would give me help.
The things I have suffered
in anguish of soul,
the pain I have felt
from scorn and from shame—
sweetest revenge would
pay for these sorrows!
I'd win back all
the good I had lost;
Indeed, I'd regain
all I had mourned for—
if I could find that dear friend
and clasp him firm in my arms!

SIEGMUND.
(*embracing her ardently*)

O, radiant one,
I am that friend

who's heir both to sword and wife!
Hot in my breast
burns now the oath
which weds me, dear one, to you.
For all I have sought
I meet now in you.
In you, loved one,
I find what I've lacked.
Shame has been yours,
and woe has been mine.
Men have despised me,
and you have been scorned.
Joyful revenge now
smiles on the happy!
I laugh out
in holy delight,
clasping you close to my bosom,
feeling the throb of your heart.

SIEGLINDA.
(in alarm, tearing herself away)

Oh, who's that? Who came just now?
(The outer door has sprung wide open. Outside the night is beautiful. The full moon shines upon the two, and all about them suddenly becomes visible.)

SIEGMUND.

No one went—
yet someone came.
See now, the spring
laughs in the hall!
(The rear door has sprung open and remains wide open. Outside is a lovely spring night. The full moon shines in on the pair.)
Storms of winter yield to
the joyful May.
The spring is shining:
mild is his light.
On gentle breezes,
light and lovely,
weaving patterns,

see him move.
Through wood and mead
his breath is stirring.
Widely open
laugh his eyes.
The blissful song of birdlings
show his voice.
Gentle perfumes
scent his breath.
From his ardent blood are blooming
beautiful flowers.
Bud and sprout
up-spring at his word.
His gently wielded rod
holds sway over earth.
Winter and storm bow to
his potent rule.
So surely no door so strong
but must yield its might to his power.
That obstinate door
once—kept us from him.
To greet his sister
swiftly he flew.
Fond love attracted the spring.
Within our bosoms,
deep it lay hid,
but now it laughs in the light.
The bride who is sister
is freed by the brother.
What kept them apart
lies broken to bits.
Joyous greetings unite the pair,
and love and spring are made one.

SIEGLINDA.

You are the spring,
the spring I have longed for
in time of the winter frost.
My heart gave you hail
with holiest awe

when at first your glance shone upon me.
All I had looked on was strange.
All that was near me was friendless,
as though all things that I met
had not ever been known.
But you, though, I
thoroughly knew.
And I knew you were mine
when I first saw you.
What was hid in my heart,
what I am,
broke on my mind,
clear as the day,
as cymbals of brass
break on the ear,
when within this frosty bleakness
at last I beheld my friend.
*(She hangs upon his neck in rapture and looks
                                    into his face.)*

SIEGMUND.

O, sweetest of raptures!
Woman most blest!

SIEGLINDA.

O, let me clasp you
and hold you near me,
that I may look on
the holy light
that from your eyes
and countenance shines,
and so sweetly masters my sense!

SIEGMUND.

The moon of spring
shines on you bright;
how attractive
your wavy hair.
At last I know
what captured my heart:
I joy in feasting my gaze.
How wide and open
gleams your brow.

Your temple displays
all the interlaced veins.
I tremble and my captive
holds me entranced.
A wonder takes my attention:
Before this first time we met
my eyes had seen your face!

SIEGMUND.

I too recall
a dream of love:
an ardent longing
brought me your sight!

SIEGLINDA.

A brook I looked in
gave back my face—
and now again I behold it:
what once the pool did reveal
now is reflected by you!

SIEGMUND.

You are the picture
long hid in my heart!

SIEGLINDA.
(quickly turning aside her gaze)

O, still! That voice!
Just let me listen!
I heard, as a child,
similar sounds.
Yet no! I heard them just lately,
when from the woods there came
the echoing peal of my voice.

SIEGMUND.

What ravishing lute tones
capture my hearing!

SIEGLINDA.
(again gazing into his eyes)

I've already seen
the glow of these eyes—
The stranger in gray
glanced at me thus,
and he thereby dispelled my woe.

By his look
his child knew the truth
and almost could give him his name.
      (She pauses, then resumes softly.)
Are you "Woe-king" indeed?

SIEGMUND.

Don't call me so.
Since you are mine,
I'm lord now of highest rapture!

SIEGLINDA.

And could you joy to
take the name "Peaceful"?

SIEGMUND.

Give me the name
that you'd love men to call me:
I'll take the name that you give!

SIEGLINDA.

And yet you called Wolfe your father?

SIEGMUND.

A wolf to the coward foxes!
This one, whose eyes
lightened as proudly
radiant one,
as yours do now,
was called—Volsa by name.

SIEGLINDA.
(beside herself)

Was Volsa your father,
and are you a Volsung?
Then it's for you—
his sword in the tree!
So let me then call you,
as I do love you,
Siegmund.
I'll call you that.

SIEGMUND.
(springing over to the tree and seizing fast the sword)
Siegmund say I,
and Siegmund am I:
bear witness this sword

I grip without shrinking!
Volsa made promise
in greatest need
this would be mine.
I hold it now!
Love that's most holy,
greatest need,
love with its longing,
need with desire,
brightly burn in my breast,
urging deeds and death!
Needful! Needful!
let that be your name—
Needful! Needful!
Sword that I need!
Show me your sharp
and cutting tooth.
Come out of the scabbard to me!
*(With mighty tug he draws the sword from
the tree and shows it to the astonished and
delighted Sieglinda.)*

Siegmund the Volsung
stands here, wife!
For bride-gift he
brings you this sword.
And thus he woos
the woman most blest.
He'll lead you from
the house of the foe.
Far from here
follow me now
out to the joyful
house of the spring:
your guard is Needful the Sword,
for Siegmund lies felled by your love.
*(He puts his arm around her to take her with
him.)*

SIEGLINDA.

Are you Siegmund
standing beside me?

Sieglinda am I,
who longed for you,
your very sister
now won the same time as the sword!

SIEGMUND.

Bride and sister
be to your brother—
Let Volsung blood bloom to the world!

(He draws her to him in passionate frenzy. She sinks to his breast with a cry.)

THE CURTAIN FALLS QUICKLY

Act Two

A Wild and Rocky Pass

In the background a gorge slopes downward from a high peak, the ground sinking again gradually from this toward the foreground.

Wotan in warlike array, is bearing his spear; before him stands Brunnhilda, fully armed as a Valkyr.

WOTAN.

Now bridle your horse,
valorous maid!
Furious strife
soon will break out.
Brunnhilda, storm to the fight,
for now the Volsung must win!
Hunding has to choose
where he will go:
I ban him now from Valhall!
So up and away!
Ride to the field!

BRUNNHILDA.
(springing from rock to rock up the height, and shouting)

Hoyotoho! Hoyotoho!
Heiaha! Heiaha!
Hahei! Hahei! Heiaho!
(She pauses on a high peak, looks down into the ravine below, and calls to Wotan.)

I warn you, father,
ready yourself,
brave the storm
blowing this way.
Fricka's coming, your wife,
She's riding in her ram-driven car.
Hei! hear the golden
whip that she cracks!
The wretched beasts are
groaning in fear.
I hear the wheels rattle.
How she rides for the brawl!
Such strife as this
is not to my taste!
Better the valorous
wars of men.
Take care, try to weather the storm.
I willingly leave you to fate!
Hoyotoho! Hoyotoho!
Heiaha! Heiaha!
Hoyotoho! Hoyotoho!
Heiaha! Heiaha!
Hoyotoho! Hoyotoho!
Hoyotoho! Hoyotoho!
Heiahaha!
*(She vanishes behind the rocks, as Fricka
enters from the heights, after ascending from
the ravine, in her chariot drawn by two rams,
alights quickly, and strides angrily toward
Wotan.)*

WOTAN.

the same old storm!
The same old woe!
And yet here I must face it.

FRICKA.

Though you hid among the hills
to miss the eyes of your wife,
still I came,
all by myself,
to get your promised assistance.

WOTAN.

Reveal your troubles,
Fricka, my love.

FRICKA.

I perceived Hunding's need.
He called me, craving revenge.
So wedding's guardian
lent her ear,
and gave pledge
to punish the deed
the bad, impudent pair
so boldly did to the spouse.

WOTAN.

Was these mortals' deed so bad
whom spring united in love?
An ardent magic
entranced the two.
I ask no amends for love.

FRICKA.

How stupid and dumb you would seem,
as though you were not aware
that when one flaunts the
holiest vows
of wedlock, I must lament it.

WOTAN.

Unholy
always the vow
that joins those that lack love.
And now truly,
do not expect
me to put a stop to
the thing you cannot,
for where keen fires are raging
I say quite frankly, just fight!

FRICKA.

Since you look lightly
on wedlock's breach,
go prattle still further,
and call it holy
that incest should bloom forth

from bond of a twin-born pair.
My heart is aghast,
my mind's in a whirl.
Wedlock unites
the sister and brother.
When has it been heard
that sister and brother did marry?

WOTAN.

So—hear of it now.
Endure then thus
what has been ordained,
though till now it has never been so.
They love one another—
that you know well—
so hear my honest advice!
If bliss is yours
as reward for your blessing,
then bless them, glad for the love that
makes these two beings as one.

FRICKA.

It reached a sad pass
with the gods everlasting,
when you begat the
violent Volsungs!
I speak plainly—
have I hit home?
You look on our lofty
race as a mockery.
You cast off all that
you once held in honor.
You've broken the bonds that
you made in the first place—
loosed while laughing
the hold of heaven,
so your silly, rascally couple,
the sensual fruit of sin,
can just revel and wanton at will.
Yet why worry for
wedlock and vows
which yourself were first to defame!

You've always wronged
your virtuous wife.
Never a depth and
never a height but
therein peeped and
lusted your look.
With an urge for change ever growing,
your scorn has harrowed my heart.
Sad were the thoughts
pent up in my bosom
when off you marched
with those wretched maidens
your lawless love had
brought to the world.
Yet you've showed such fear of your wife
that the Valkyrie band,
and Brunnhild herself—
who is near your heart—
you have ordered to listen to me.
But now that new names have
taken your fancy,
you roam the forest
as Volsa the wolfish!
Then when you've sunk to the
depths of your shame,
you beget a couple
of commonplace mortals.
Now the wife of your vows
is flung at the feet of your whelps!
So finish your work!
Fill up my cup:
The betrayed one now must be trampled!

WOTAN.
(*calmly*)

You've never learned—
though I would teach you—
the things you can't comprehend,
for first they have to take place.
All you know is

the commonplace things,
whereas my thoughts foresee
the events yet to come.
One thing, mark you:
need brings a man
who, free from godly protection,
is free from the laws of the gods.
Only such can
accomplish the deed,
which, though gods would perform it,
no god dare perform for himself.

FRICKA.

Your thoughts are deep and
meant to confuse me.
What lofty deed can
hero accomplish
that by the gods is not to be done,
by whose grace alone he can work?

WOTAN.

And his own plain courage
counts not at all?

FRICKA.

Who breathed the life into men,
gave light to who hardly could see.
They seem quite strong,
aided by you,
and when you goad them,
truly they strive.
You—you alone goad them.
The god then says they are good!
With new deceits
you would still evade me,
with new devices
still would outrun me.
And yet this Volsung
shall never be yours.
I can strike you through him.
He is bold only through you.

WOTAN.

His woes were wild,
and he grew by himself.
My arm shielded him not.

FRICKA.

Then shield him not today.
Take back the sword
you gave to him once.

WOTAN.

The sword?

FRICKA.

Yes, the sword,
that ready sword,
magic in might,
that you, god, did grant your son.

WOTAN.

Siegmund achieved it himself
in his need.

FRICKA.

You shaped both his need
and the sword of his need.
Would you deceive me,
who day and night
followed close on your heels?
For him you did thrust
the sword in the tree,
and you promised him
the noble steel.
Can you deny it
was only your art
that brought him where it was found?
A noble will
fight not a vassal.
Such rogues are only for whipping.
Fight against your force:
that I might do;
but Siegmund is only a knave.
Shall he who owes you
service and homage
be master now

of the goddess, your wife?
Shall one so base
outrageously shame me,
a varlet dictate,
a ruler obey?
My husband cannot desire it.
He would not dishonor his queen.

WOTAN.

What then would you?

FRICKA.

Give up the Volsung.

WOTAN.
(with choked voice)

He goes his own way.

FRICKA.

Why then—give him no aid,
when the foe calls for vengeance due.

WOTAN.

I'll—give him no aid.

FRICKA.

Look at me plainly.
Plan no deceit.
Just keep Brunnhild out of his way.

WOTAN.

The Valkyrie rules herself.

FRICKA.

Not yet. It is your will
alone she obeys.
Forbid her to help him win.

WOTAN.

I cannot destroy him:
he found my sword.

FRICKA.

Get rid of the magic,
his weapon will break.
Let him fight without arms!

BRUNNHILDA'S VOICE.
Heiaha! Heiaha!

Hoyotoho!
*(The Valkyrie appears with her steed on the
rocky path.)*

FRICKA.

Here comes your audacious maid.
Hear the joy in her voice!

BRUNNHILDA.

Heiaha! Heiaha!
Hoyohotoyo hotoyoha!

WOTAN.
(aside)

I called her for Siegmund to horse.

FRICKA.

Let her shield today
protect the fair honor
of Wotan's holy wife.
A mock to mankind,
and shorn of our might,
even we gods will be doomed,
if this day your valiant
maid fails to champion
my high and legitimate rights.
Your son must die for my honor.
Will Wotan so pledge me his oath?

WOTAN.
*(throwing himself upon a rocky seat in utter dejection and
inward rage)*

Take the oath!
*(Brunnhilda, perceiving Fricka, suddenly
breaks off her song and leads her horse by
the bridle quietly and slowly down the mountain path. She hides the steed in a cave just
as Fricka passes her on her way back to her
chariot.)*

FRICKA.
(to Brunnhilda)

Lord father
waits for you.
Let him inform you
how the lot has been cast.
(She mounts her car and drives off.)

BRUNNHILDA.
*(Advances with anxious and wondering look toward Wotan,
who, head on hand, is absorbed in gloomy reflection.)*

> Ill, likely,
> soon will come:
> Fricka laughed at the outcome.
> Father, what must your child experience?
> Crushed you seem, and unhappy.

WOTAN.

> The chains I welded
> now hold me fast—
> least free of all beings.

BRUNNHILDA.

> You never were thus.
> What gnaws at your heart?

WOTAN.

> O, greatest of shame!
> O, shamefulest woe!
> Gods have grief!
> Gods have grief!
> Infinite wrath!
> Endless despair!
> The saddest I am of all beings!

BRUNNHILDA.
*(In alarm, throws away her shield, spear and helmet, and sinks
at Wotan's feet.)*

> Father! Father!
> Tell me, what is it?
> You are filling your child with alarm!
> Have trust in me,
> your daughter true.
> See, Brunnhild is pleading.
> *(She lays her head and hands confidingly and
> anxiously on his knees and breast.)*

WOTAN.
*(Gazes long into her face and strokes her hair. Then, as if com-
ing to himself again, he at last begins in a very low voice.)*

> Yet if I tell it,
> might I not lose
> the controlling power of my will?

BRUNNHILDA.

To Wotan's will you're speaking,
telling me what you will.
What am I,
if I am not your will?

WOTAN.

What never was uttered to any
will stay unuttered,
now and forever.
Myself I speak to,
speaking to you.
When young love vanished
with its delights,
my spirit aspired to power,
and spurred by former
wishes, I went
and won myself the world.
I thought no falsehood,
yet I did falsely,
carried out contracts
where harm lay hid.
Wandering Loge did lure me,
then left me in the lurch.
But the urge for love
still had some power.
In my might I longed for affection.
In night was born
the fearsome Nibelung.
Alberich broke through its law,
by cursing at love;
so he won through the curse
the glittering gold of the Rhine,
and with it measureless might.
I ravished the ring
he cunningly fashioned
yet it did not
go back to the Rhine:
with it I paid for
Valhall's ramparts,

the fort the giants have built me,
from which I hold rule of the world.
The one who knows
all things that were,
Erda, the wisest
holiest Vala,
warned me off from the ring,
told me of doom that was coming.
I desired to know more
of this future;
but silent, she vanished away.
Then I lost all my peace of mind.
The god was still eager to know.
To the womb of the earth
downward did I go:
with love's strong magic
conquered the Vala,
toppled her wisdom's pride,
so she told me what would come.
Tidings I heard from her lips:
I gave her a token while there:
most wise woman on earth,
she bore me, Brunnhilda—you.
and eight sisters
grew up with you
with such Valkyrs, I
hoped to break
the fate which the Vala
had bade me dread—
the gods' ignominious downfall.
I wanted might
to conquer the foe,
so you were sent to find heroes:
the men we once ruled
by our laws, so proudly,
the men, whose courage
we curbed and suppressed,
whom through cloudy, deceitful,
villainous compacts

we bound to a blind and
a servile obedience—
your work is to spur
and prick on their valor,
and by that rouse them
to savage war,
so valiant warrior troops may
be marshaled in Valhall's hall.

BRUNNHILDA.

We have filled Valhall with heroes;
many I brought you myself.
So why are you troubled?
We never let up.

WOTAN.

It's something else—
mark my words well—
something the Vala foretold!
For Alberich's host
threatens our downfall:
the envious dwarf
mutters with rancor;
and yet I've no fear
of his armies of darkness,
for my heroes make me secure.
But if once the ring
were won by the Nibelung—
then would our Valhall be ended.
He who curses love, he,
he alone
knows the magic
the ring possesses,
and so can will
the doom of the gods.
He seeks to turn
my heroes from me,
and when he wins
my men to his will,
to urge them on
to battle with me.

Anguish taught me the way
to wrest the ring from his clutches.
I gave a giant
payment one time
with accursed gold
for work he did.
Fafner guards now the hoard
he won from the brother he slew.
I must get the circlet from him,
which I myself used to pay him.
But I honor my word,
so dare not attack him.
Mightless by law,
my spirit is gone.
These are the fetters
that now bind me.
I who by treaties was lord,
by these treaties now am a slave.
Yet one can manage
what I don't dare,
a hero, never
helped by my power;
who, strange to gods, is
free of their grace;
on his own,
not at their beck,
his need his own,
and his arms his own—
this one can do
what I fear to try,
and never urged him do.
though it was all of my wish.
One who'd battle the god,
yet would serve me,
a favorable foe—
ah, where is he found?
How bring forth a freeman
I've never aided,
who despite defiance

is dear to my heart?
Now could I create one
who not through me,
but through himself would
express my will?
O, need of the gods!
terrible shame!
I feel disgust just
seeing myself
in all the deeds I accomplish!
The other, that I have longed for,
the other I never see.
The free are their only creators—
Varlets are all I can make!

BRUNNHILDA.

Yet the Volsung, Siegmund,
is he not free?

WOTAN.

Both together
we roamed the forest.
Boldly, I brought him up to
flaunt the laws of the gods—
only the sword can save him
now from the wrath of the gods,
and that, in favor,
came from a god!
Why did I want to
trick myself this way?
How easily Fricka
found out the fraud!
She saw right through me,
all to my shame!
I must yield my will to her purpose.

BRUNNHILDA.

So Siegmund must fall in the fight?

WOTAN.
(in a frenzy of despair)

I have handled Alberich's ring—
grasped the gold in my greed!

The curse that I fled
will flee not from me.
What I love I now must surrender,
murder what most I've cherished,
basely betray the
one who trusts!
Farewell to you,
glorious pomp,
godly pretense's
glittering shame!
So let it perish—
all I have built!
So I end my work,
and wait for just one thing:
the finish—
the finish!

(He pauses in meditation.)

And for that finish
looks Alberich!
Now I've fathomed
the secret sense
of Vala's maddening riddle:
"When the darksome foe of love
wrathful, brings forth a son,
the blest one's end
will linger not!"
A rumor told
a tale of the dwarf,
that he'd won himself a woman,
his gold gaining her grace.
The fruit of hate
soon is to come.
The seed of spite
grows in her womb.
This wonder befell
the loveless Nibelung!
But I have never brought forth
a free one, although I have loved.

(grimly)

So take of my blessing,
Nibelungen son!
What deeply grieves me
is yours to inherit;
my godhood's empty display;
so gnaw away, glutting your greed.

BRUNNHILDA.
(*in terror*)

O, say, tell me,
what must your child do?

WOTAN.
(*bitterly*)

Fight strictly for Fricka,
guard holy wedlock's laws!
The choice she made,
is also my own.
The will that I work is worthless,
for my will can't bring forth a free man.
Help Fricka's vassals
when there is strife!

BRUNNHILDA.

Woe! Have pity!
Retract your words!
You love Siegmund.
For your sake—
I know it—I shall protect him.

WOTAN.

Put an end to Siegmund,
for Hunding must win in the strife.
Watch yourself well,
maintain your control.
Put forth your prowess
to further his fight.
A charmed sword
helps Siegmund.
Strength and valor is his!

BRUNNHILDA.

One you have taught me
always to love
who in lofty virtue

is dear to your bosom
never will find me hostile
through your two-faced word!

WOTAN.

Ha, shameless one!
This is your taunt?
Who are you, if not the blind and
tame tool of my will?
When I told my sorrows
did I so sink
as to be a mock to
the being I made?
Does my child know my wrath?
Your spirit would quail
if I were ever
to hurl bolts of my fire!
Within my bosom
smoulders a hate
which could send forth
horrors on the world
that once was all my delight.
Woe to him whom it hits!
Grief would pay for his pride!
So heed my words.
Rouse me not up.
Be sure you hark to my hest:
death to Siegmund!
This be the Valkyrie's work.
(*He storms away, vanishing in the
                                    mountains.*)

BRUNNHILDA.

Father was
never like this,
although he oft was quick in wrath.
                    (*She stands a while stunned.*)
How heavy
my weapons' weight!
When I loved the fight,
how light they did seem!

This evil strife
makes me fear my task!

> *(She ponders and sighs.)*

Woe, my Volsung!
In greatest need
I must falsely abandon the true one!

*(She looks up to see Siegmund and Sieglinda
ascending from the gorge. She watches them
a moment and then re-enters the cave to her
horse. Siegmund and Sieglinda enter. She
presses hastily forward; he seeks to restrain
her.)*

SIEGMUND.

Rest here a while;
take some repose!

SIEGLINDA.

Onward! Onward!

SIEGMUND.
(putting his arm around her, firmly but tenderly)

No farther now!
Just wait, O sweetest of wives!
You start from the rapture
love would arouse,
with sudden haste
hurrying forth,
so fast I can scarce pursue;
through wood and plain,
over rock and stone,
speechless, silent,
bounding along.
No call kept you from flight.

> *(She stares wildly into vacancy.)*

Rest for a while,
say just a word,
ending your silent woe!
See, your brother
holds you, his bride—
Siegmund now is your mate!

(He has led her quietly to the rocky seat.)

SIEGLINDA.

(gazes into Siegmund's eyes with growing rapture, then mournfully hangs upon his neck. Then she starts up in sudden panic, while Siegmund tries to hold her.)

Away! Away!
Flee the profaned one!
Unholy
the clasp of her arm.
Disgraced, dishonored,
let me stay dead!
Flee this body,
let it alone!
May winds blow her away,
the foul one who followed the fair!
For he has given her love,
and blessedest joy was hers.
She loved her lover in full,
who gave in full of his love.
In the sweetest delights of
holiest raptures,
a piercing pain
struck senses and soul;
groanings and shudders
of shame and of terror
fastened their grip
and filled her with horror
to think she once had obeyed
a man she loved not at all!
Leave the accursed,
leave her to flee!
An outcast am I,
bereft of grace!
I now must leave him
the purest of manhood,
I dare not be yours
in love and obedience:
Shame would fall on my brother,
scorn on rescuing friend!

SIEGMUND.

For all shame you have felt
the blood of the vile shall pay!
So flee now no farther.
Wait for the foeman.
Here—here I shall slay him:
when Needful's point
shall taste his heart.
Vengeance shall surely be yours!

SIEGLINDA.
(starting up and listening)

Hark! The horn-calls—
Listen—those sounds!
All around,
raging and shrill
from wood and vale
clamors arise.
Hunding has wakened
from heavy sleep.
Kinsmen and bloodhounds have
come as he calls them.
Hear how the pack
howls in frenzy,
loud-baying to heaven
at the breaking of wedlock's fair vows!
(She laughs wildly, then suddenly shrinks in
terror.)

Where are you, Siegmund?
Are you still here?
Ardently loved and
radiant brother!
Let your starlit eyes
shine once more on me sweetly.
Spurn not the kiss
of the outcast, loving wife!
Hark! O, hark!
That is Hunding's horn!
Hear his hounds come near
in mighty force!

No sword serves
when the pack attacks.
Drop your blade, Siegmund!
Siegmund—where are you?
Ah, there—I see you there—
Terrible sight!
Bloodhounds gnashing
their ravening fangs!
They pay no heed
to your noble glance.
And they maul your feet with
their terrible teeth—
You fall—
In pieces now lies your sword!
The ashtree splits—
its trunk is riven.
Brother! My brother!
Siegmund, ha!
(She shrieks and falls senseless into Sieg-
mund's arms.)

SIEGMUND.

Sister! Beloved!
(He listens for her breathing until he knows
that she still lives. He lowers her gently, seats
himself, and rests her head on his knee. After
a pause he bends tenderly over her, and im-
presses a long kiss on her brow.)

BRUNNHILDA.
(leading her steed by the bridle, enters slowly from the cave
and advances solemnly. On nearing Siegmund she halts. She
bears her shield and spear in one hand, rests the other on her
horse's neck, and remains in this attitude, silently and earnestly
observing Siegmund.)

Siegmund!
Look at me!
I'm—one
you follow soon.

SIEGMUND.
(raising his eyes)

Who are you, say,
who appear so solemn and fair?

BRUNNHILDA.

The doomed to death
alone may see me.
Who views my form
must part with the light of life.
On the war-plain alone
the valiant see me.
He whom I meet
is chosen for his doom.

SIEGMUND.

When you lead on,
whither follows the hero?

BRUNNHILDA.

To Val-father.
You are his choice.
Follow me.
To Valhall we must go.

SIEGMUND.

In Valhall does
Val-father live by himself?

BRUNNHILDA.

His noble host
of heroes slain
will throng you round
and give greetings most high.

SIEGMUND.

Then shall I find in
Valhall, my father Volsa?

BRUNNHILDA.

You'll find your father
the Volsung there.

SIEGMUND.

Say, will a woman
greet me with joy?

BRUNNHILDA.

Wish-maids divine

will tend you.
Wotan's daughter too
will proffer you drink.

SIEGMUND.

You are high:
I know you as holy
Lord Wotan's child.
Yet one thing tell me, Immortal!
Will brother take with him
his bride who is sister?
Will Siegmund clasp
Sieglinda there?

BRUNNHILDA.

Earthly air
must she keep breathing
Think not to
find Sieglinda there!

SIEGMUND.

Then greet for me Valhall,
hail for me Wotan,
hail for me Volsa
and all the heroes—
hail too the fair and
gracious wish-maids.
I will not follow you there.

BRUNNHILDA.

You've looked on the Valkyrie's
withering glance:
you must follow her now!

SIEGMUND.

Where Sieglinda lives
in joy and woe,
there will Siegmund live also.
My looks have not paled,
yet still I see you,
You cannot force me to go!

BRUNNHILDA.

While life is yours
be your own lord.
But then, O fool, death must rule.

I am his herald,
so have come.

SIEGMUND.

What hero today
shall lay me low?

BRUNNHILDA.

This day Hunding must win.

SIEGMUND.

Bring stronger menace
than Hunding's warfare!
Lurk if you like,
looking for spoil.
Choose this man for your prey:
I think he will fall in the fight.

BRUNNHILDA.
(shaking her head)

You, Volsung,
hear what I say!
Such is your coming fate.

SIEGMUND.

Look at this sword!
Its might was made
that I might win.
I defy your threats with this blade.

BRUNNHILDA.

He who contrived it
dooms you to death.
He has cast the spell from the sword.

SIEGMUND.
(angrily)

Peace! Alarm not
my slumbering bride!
Woe! Woe; Sweetest of wives!
You saddest among all the faithful!
All the world
rages around you
and I whom alone you did trust,
for whom you defied all the world—
I cannot save,
or give my protection—

for what can I do but betray?
O, shame on him
who bestowed the sword,
who makes of my triumph scorn!
If I must perish,
I'll fare not to Valhall,
Hella pleases me more.

BRUNNHILDA.

You think so little of
heavenly rapture.
One poor woman
to you is all,
who, tired and ailing,
feebly reclines in your arms.
Is she all you hold dear?

SIEGMUND.

So young and fair
you shine to my eyes:
yet how cold and hard,
seen by my heart.
If you can only
show scorn, then be gone,
you wretched, feelingless maid!
But if you must feed on
this woe of mine,
why then, rejoice if you will.
Let my woe pleasure your envious heart.
But of Valhall's brittle raptures,
vaunt no vauntings of them.

BRUNNHILDA.

I know all the pain
that is gnawing your heart;
I feel for the hero's
sacred despair
Siegmund, entrust her to me;
I'll keep her safe in my care!

SIEGMUND.

No other than I
is to touch this purest of women;

and if I must die
I shall slay her first as she sleeps!

BRUNNHILDA.

Volsung! Reckless one!
Hear my advice:
entrust me your wife
for the pledge she gladly
received when you gave of your love!

SIEGMUND.
(drawing his sword)

This sword—
which a false man once made for a true;
this sword—
a coward when facing the foe,
useless when turned on the foe,
is useful when turned on the friend!
(He holds the sword over Sieglinda.)
Two lives now
laugh at you here.
Take them, Needful,
envious steel!
Take them at one fell stroke!

BRUNNHILDA.

Forbear, Volsung!
Siegmund shall live—
this is my promise—
and Sieglind also shall live!
The word is said.
Your fate is altered.
You, Siegmund,
take my blessing and win.
(A horn is heard in the distance.)
Hark to the horn!
Now, hero, prepare!
Trust to the sword,
and swing it assured.
Your weapon's as true
as the Valkyr is true in pledge!
Farewell, Siegmund,
hero most blest!

We shall meet once more at the battle!

(She hastens away, disappearing with her horse in a ravine. Siegmund follows her with his eyes, seeming elated. Meanwhile it has grown dark. Heavy thunderclouds hide the hills, the ravine and the lofty rocks. Distant horn-calls continue to be heard and through the following scene gradually grow louder.)

SIEGMUND.
(bending over Sieglinda)

Slumber's charm
has softly soothed
my fair one's pain and grief.
When the Valkyrie met my path
did she bring this blissful repose?
Should not the carnage of war
have frightened a suffering wife?
Lifeless seems she,
and yet she lives.
The sad one has found
a beautiful dream.

(new horn-call)

So slumber right on
till the fight is fought,
and peace has brought you joy.
(He lays her gently on the rocky seat, kisses her brow, and, after the horns have been heard again, makes ready to go.)
You there who call,
ready yourself.
Soon he shall have
what is due
Needful knows what to pay!
(He hastens to the back and disappears in the black mists on the mountain peak.)

SIEGLINDA.
(dreaming)

Father, come back to our home!
He still dwells in the woods
with the boy.

Mother! Mother!
My courage fails!
The strangers seem not
friendly and peaceful.
Clouds of blackness—
fumes that oppress—
fiery flames are
licking our way.
They burn the house!
Come and help me, brother!
Siegmund! Siegmund!
(Vivid lightning breaks through the clouds.
A fearful thunderclap following awakes Sieg-
linda suddenly.)

Siegmund! Ah!
(She stares around her in terror. Thunder-
clouds gather and from all sides are heard
approaching horn-calls.)

HUNDING'S VOICE.
(from the peak)

Woe-king! Woe-king!
Stay for the fight!
Or shall my hounds come and stop you?

SIEGMUND'S VOICE.
(heard in the distance from the ravine)

Where have you hid,
that I may swoop on you?
Stay and let me face you!

SIEGLINDA.
(listening, horror-struck)

Hunding—Siegmund—
Could I but see them!

HUNDING'S VOICE.

Come here, you rascally suitor!
Fricka waits for you here!

SIEGMUND'S VOICE.
(now also on the rocky peak)

You think me still weaponless,
craven rogue!
Threat not with women,

but fight unaided,
else think not Fricka will help!
For see, from the tree that
grows in your house
I drew, undaunted, the sword.
(A lightning flash lighting up the crag, momentarily reveals Hunding and Siegmund fighting.)

SIEGLINDA.

Stay your hands, you foemen!
Murder me first!
(She rushes toward the peak, but so violent a lightning flash breaks that she staggers back blinded. In the glare Brunnhilda is seen, soaring over Siegmund and covering him with her shield.)

BRUNNHILDA'S VOICE.

Slay him, Siegmund!
Trust in your sword!
(Just as Siegmund aims a deadly blow at Hunding a reddish glow breaks through the clouds, heralding Wotan, who stands above Hunding and points his spear at Siegmund.)

WOTAN.

Get back from the spear!
In pieces the sword!
(Brunnhilda, with her shield, has recoiled in terror. Siegmund's sword is shivered on the outstretched spear; Hunding buries his sword in Siegmund's breast. Siegmund falls. Sieglinda, hearing his dying groan, falls senseless. The glow then vanishes and the lightning stops. Darkness enshrouds the scene. Brunnhilda, dimly visible, hastens to the assistance of Sieglinda.)

BRUNNHILDA.

To horse, that I may save you!
(She lifts Sieglinda on to the horse which stands in the defile close by and immediately disappears with her. The clouds part in the midst and show clearly Hunding withdrawing his sword from the fallen foe. Wotan,

*surrounded by clouds, stands behind him on
a rock, leaning on his spear and gazing sorrowfully on Siegmund's body.)*

WOTAN.

Away, knave!
Kneel before Fricka
Tell her that Wotan's spear
avenged what brought her shame.
Go! Go!
*(He makes a contemptuous gesture with his
hand and Hunding falls dead.)*
But Brunnhilda—
woe to that criminal!
Fearful shall
her punishment be
if once I reach her in flight!
(He vanishes amid thunder and lightning.)

QUICK CURTAIN

ACT THREE

The Summit of a Rocky Mountain

To the right, a forest of fir trees. Left, the entrance to a cave. Above this the rock rises high. At back the view is uninterrupted. Rocks of various sizes form an embankment to the precipice. Occasional clouds fly past the summit, storm-swept.

Gerhilda, Ortlinda, Valtrauta and Schwertleita, Valkyrie maidens, are ensconsed on the rocky peak above the cave. They are in full armor.

GERHILDA.
(Higher placed than the rest, calls toward the back.)
> Ho-yo-to-ho! Ho-yo-to-ho!
> Hi-ya-ha! Hi-ya-ha!
> Helmviga, here!
> Hie here with your horse!
> *(A flash of lightning breaks through a passing cloud: a Valkyrie on horseback is visible in it: over her saddle hangs a slain warrior.)*

HELMVIGA'S VOICE.
> Ho-yo-to-ho! Ho-yo-to-ho!
> Ho-yo-to-ho! Ho-yo-to-ho!
> Hi-ya-ha!

GERHILDA,
VALTRAUTA &
SCHWERTLEITA.
> Hi-ya-ha! Hi-ya-ha!
> *(The cloud with the apparition disappears behind a fir tree on the right.)*

129

ORTLINDA.
(shouting in the direction of the fir tree)
> Your stallion should be by
> Ortlinda's mare.
> My Gray is glad to
> graze with your Brownie.

VALTRAUTA.
> Who hangs from your saddle?

HELMVIGA.
(stepping from the fir trees)
> Sintolt the Hegeling!

SCHWERTLEITA.
> Lead off your Brownie
> far from my gray one.
> Ortlinda's mare now
> bears Wittig, the Irming!

GERHILDA.
> As foemen I saw just
> Sintolt and Wittig.

ORTLINDA.
(suddenly darting over to the fir tree)
> Hi-ya-ha! Hi-ya-ha! Your horse
> is butting my mare!

SCHWERTLEITA
& GERHILDA.
(laughing)
> The warriors' strife
> makes foes of the horses.

HELMVIGA.
(into the trees)
> Quiet, Brownie!
> Peaceful does it!

VALTRAUTA.
(who has taken the place of Gerhilda at the top of the peak)
> Ho-yo-ho! Ho-yo-ho!
> Siegruna, here!
> Where were you so long?
> *(Siegruna rides by, as Helmviga did, in the
> direction of the fir tree.)*

SIEGRUNA'S VOICE.

Work to do!
Are the others all here?

THE VALKYRIES.

Ho-yo-to-ho! Ho-yo-to-ho!
Hi-ya-ha! Hi-ya-ha!
*(Siegruna disappears behind the firs. Two
voices are heard from the depths.)*

GRIMGERDA &
ROSSVEISSA.

Ho-yo-to-ho! Ho-yo-to-ho!
Hi-ya-ha! Hi-ya-ha!

VALTRAUTA.

Rossveissa and Grimgerda!

GERHILDA.

They ride as a pair.
*(Ortlinda has returned from the fir trees with
Helmviga and the newly arrived Siegruna: all
three signal from the edge of the precipice
toward the depth.)*

ORTLINDA,
HELMVIGA &
SIEGRUNA.

Hello, you travelers!
Rossveissa and Grimgerda!

ALL THE OTHER
VALKYRIES.

Ho-yo-to-ho! Ho-yo-to-ho!
Hi-ya-ha! Hi-ya-ha!
*(Grimgerda and Rossveissa, on horseback,
appear in a glowing thundercloud which as-
cends from the depths and vanishes behind
the fir tree. Each carries a slain warrior at
her saddlebow.)*

GERHILDA.

Your steeds to the forest
for feed and rest!

ORTLINDA.

Tether the mares
away from each other,

until our heroes'
hate is allayed!

HELMVIGA.
(amid the laughter of her companions)
The gray has paid
for wrath of the heroes!
(Grimgerda and Rossveissa issue from the
fir trees.)

THE VALKYRIES.
Valkyries, you're welcome!

SCHWERTLEITA.
Did you come as a pair?

GRIMGERDA.
We rode singly first,
encountered today.

ROSSVEISSA.
If we all are assembled,
let's wait no longer:
to Valhall let us be off,
bringing the slain to our lord

HELMVIGA.
Eight are we here,
one we still lack.

GERHILDA.
Brunnhilda still is waiting,
tending the Volsung.

VALTRAUTA.
Then we must tarry
here till she comes.
Father would give us
greeting most grim,
should he not see her with us.

SIEGRUNA.
(from the rocky peak where she is looking out)
Ho-yo-to-ho! Ho-yo-to-ho!
Look here! Look here!
She's coming here now
in galloping haste!

THE VALKYRIES.
(hurrying toward the summit)

> Hi-ya-ha! Ho-yo-to-ho! Ho-yo-to-ho!
> Brunnhilda! Hi!

VALTRAUTA.

> With her tired horse see
> her head for the pines.

GRIMGERDA.

> The fast journey
> makes Grane snort!

ROSSVEISSA.

> No Valkyr before
> ever so galloped!

ORTLINDA.

> What lies on her saddle?

HELMVIGA.

> That is no man!

SIEGRUNA.

> It's a maid, truly.

GERHILDA.

> Then where was she found?

SCHWERTLEITA.

> She quite refrains
> greeting her sisters.

VALTRAUTA.

> Hi-ya-ha! Brunnhilda!
> Can you not hear?

ORTLINDA.

> Help our sister
> off from the saddle!

THE VALKYRIES.

> Ho-yo-to-ho! Ho-yo-to-ho!
> Hi-ya-ha! Hi-ya-ha!
> *(Gerhilda and Helmviga head for the fir*
> *trees.)*

VALTRAUTA.

> But Grane the stalwart has fallen.
> *(Siegruna and Valtrauta follow the two*
> *others.)*

GRIMGERDA

    See her lift the maid
    from saddle to earth.

THE OTHER VALKYRIES.
(Hurrying toward the fir trees)

    Sister. Sister!
    What has occurred?
    (They all re-enter. With them comes Brunn-
        hilda supporting and leading Sieglinda.)

BRUNNHILDA.

    Shield me, and help,
    my need is dire!

THE VALKYRIES.

    From whence do you ride
    in furious haste?
    So gallop those who must flee!

BRUNNHILDA.

    I flee for the first time,
    and am pursued!
    Lord-father dogs my heels!

THE VALKYRIES.

    Have you your senses?
    Speak to us!
    What?
    Does father follow you?
    Why do you flee?

BRUNNHILDA.

    O, sisters, look
    from the rocky summit.
    Look out northward,
    to see if he comes.
    (Ortlinda and Valtrauta spring up to watch
                      from the peak.)
    Quick! What do you see?

ORTLINDA.

    A thunderstorm
    nears from northward.

VALTRAUTA.

    Gathering clouds
    congregate there.

THE VALKYRIES.

>War-father's riding
>his heavenly steed!

BRUNNHILDA.

>The wild pursuer
>draws near from the north!
>He nears, he rides and rages!
>Shield me, sisters!
>Keep her from harm!

THE VALKYRIES.

>What's wrong with the woman?

BRUNNHILDA.

>Hark to me quickly!
>Sieglinda is she,
>Siegmund's sister and bride.
>Wotan is raging
>against the Volsungen pair.
>He told me to withdraw
>from the brother
>victory in strife.
>But with my shield
>I kept him from harm,
>braving the god,
>who struck him himself with his spear.
>Siegmund fell.
>But I flew
>far with the bride,
>and to save her
>hastened to you,
>if your fears would let
>you hide her from the punishing blow.

THE VALKYRIES.

>O, foolish sister!
>What have you done?
>Sorrow! Sorrow!
>Brunnhilda, sorrow!
>Did disobedient
>Brunnhilda
>break father's holy command?

VALTRAUTA.
(from the height)

Night is drawing
quite near from the north.

ORTLINDA.

Heading hither
rages the storm.

SIEGRUNA.

Wild neighs come
from father's steed!
Hear it snorting this way!

BRUNNHILDA.

Woe to this sufferer
when Wotan arrives,
to all of the Volsungs
threatening destruction.
Who's here that will lend
her fleetest of steeds,
to help the woman escape?

SIEGRUNA.

Would you have us
rashly rebel?

BRUNNHILDA.

Rossveissa, sister
let me have your courser!

ROSSVEISSA.

The fleet one has never
fled from our lord.

BRUNNHILDA.

Helmviga, listen!

HELMVIGA.

I listen to father.

BRUNNHILDA.

Grimgerda! Gerhilda!
Lend me your horse!
Schwertleita! Siegruna!
See my distress!
Be true to me,
as I have been true.
Rescue this woman of woe!

SIEGLINDA.
(who till now has stared darkly into space, starts up as Brunn-hilda puts her arm about her protectingly.)

> O suffer no sorrow for me:
> death is all that I want!
> Who bade you, maid,
> to lead me from danger?
> Much better had I
> received the stroke
> from the very weapon
> that felled my love.
> That way I would have
> been one with him.
> Far from Siegmund—
> Siegmund, from you!
> O, cover me, Death,
> from remembrance!
> Is not my flight
> good reason to curse you?
> So I beg you, hark to my prayer—
> bury your sword in my heart.

BRUNNHILDA.

> Woman, live on,
> just as love would have you.
> Rescue the pledge
> you received from his love:
> a Volsung grows in your womb.

SIEGLINDA.
(gives a violent start, then suddenly her face beams with a sublime joy.)

> Rescue me, brave one!
> Rescue my child!
> Shield me, you maidens,
> with mightiest shield!
> *(Terrible thunderclaps are heard in the distance, then they grow louder.)*

VALTRAUTA.
(from the height)

> The storm gathers fast.

ORTLINDA.

Flee, you who fear it!

THE VALKYRIES.

Hence with the woman,
Woe's in her wake.
No Valkyr would dare to
hold her from harm.

SIEGLINDA.
(*on her knees before Brunnhilda*)

Rescue me, maid!
Rescue the mother!

BRUNNHILDA.

Then flee with all swiftness,
and flee by yourself.
I'll—stay where I am,
waiting for Wotan's vengeance,
and then bearing
the brunt of his wrath
giving you time to run from his rage.

SIEGLINDA.

Where may I safely travel?

BRUNNHILDA.

Which of you, sisters,
knows what lies eastward?

SIEGRUNA.

Far hence, due east,
stretches a wood.
The Nibelung hoard
was brought by Fafner therein.

SCHWERTLEITA.

There he did turn
into a dragon;
and in a cave he
broods over Alberich's ring.

GRIMGERDA.

An uncanny place
for a helpless bride.

BRUNNHILDA.

And yet within those woods

Wotan's wrath cannot reach.
Our mighty father
avoids them with fear.

VALTRAUTA.

Wrathful, Wotan
rides to the rock!

THE VALKYRIES.

Brunnhilda, hear
how he comes with a roar!

BRUNNHILDA.
(pointing the way to Sieglinda)

Off then, quickly,
and head toward the east!
Bold in defiance,
endure every trial,
hunger and thirst,
briers and stones.
Laugh, whether need
or suffering gnaws.
For one thing know,
and know it ever:
the world's most glorious hero
lives, O woman,
and grows in your womb!
*(She takes the pieces of Siegmund's sword
from under her breastplate and gives them
to Sieglinda.)*

Guard well for his sake
these broken pieces.
Where his father perished
I luckily found them.
Who swings this sword
when forged anew
may take the name that I give—
Siegfried the victor shall thrive.

SIEGLINDA.

You noblest wonder!
Glorious maid!
My thanks for bringing
holiest balm!

For him whom we loved
I save the beloved.
May my thanks someday
bless and repay!
Fare you well!
Be blest in Sieglinda's woe!
*(She hastens away. The rocky heights are
veiled in black thunderclouds. A terrible
storm is gathering. A lurid glow appears in
the fir trees. Between peals of thunder
Wotan's voice is heard.)*

WOTAN'S VOICE.

Stay! Brunnhilda!

THE VALKYRIES.

The rock's been reached by
horse and rider.
Woe! Brunnhilda!
Vengeance has come!

BRUNNHILDA.

Ah, sisters, help!
My heart is faint!
His wrath will blast me
unless you shelter me now.

THE VALKYRIES.

Come here, you lost one!
Keep out of sight!
Cling quite close to us.
Say nothing when called!
*(All ascend to the top of the peak, concealing
Brunnhilda.)*

Woe!
Wotan wildly
leaps from his horse—
here he comes,
revenge in his stride!
*(Wotan, in a frenzy, emerges from the firs
and halts at the foot of the height on which
the Valkyries are grouped, hiding Brunnhilda.)*

WOTAN.

Where is Brunnhilda?
Where is the criminal?
Dare you to hide
the guilty from vengeance?

THE VALKYRIES.

Loud are your cries of anger!
O father, what have your daughters,
done to arouse you
to furious rage?

WOTAN.

Must you thus scorn me?
Watch yourselves, vixens!
I know: Brunnhilda's
hiding from me.
Shrink from the maid,
one cast off forever,
who by herself
cast off her worth!

THE VALKYRIES.

She came here because followed,
and with tears pleaded for aid,
Fear and trembling
grip the pursued one.
For our fearful sister
humbly we sue,
that you tame the anger you feel.

WOTAN.

Weak-spirited,
womanish brood!
Are feeble hearts
the fruit of my loins?
Was this why I made you
zealous for war,
giving you hearts
that are hard and sharp,
just to have you make moans and groans
when my anger is turned on a wretch?
So learn then, whimperers,

just what she did,
for which you weaklings
have poured out your tears.
No one as she
knew all my innermost thinking;
No one as she
fathomed the spring of my motives;
herself was
the desire that fashioned my deeds.
and now she tramples
the holiest tie,
and breaks all faith
in despite of my will,
and openly scorns
what I command,
and against me threats with the spear
that she bore by Wotan's wish!
Hear me, Brunnhilda?
You, to whom corslet,
helm and arms,
favor and joy,
being and honor were lent?
Hearing the plaint I am raising,
You seem to fear the plaintiff
as coward who flees her fate!

BRUNNHILDA.
*(Brunnhilda comes forward out of the band of the Valkyries
and moves with humble but firm steps down the rock to within
a short distance from her father.)*

Here am I, Father:
I ask to be punished.

WOTAN.

I—punish you not:
You yourself have punished yourself.
My will alone
awoke you to life,
yet your will was willed against mine.
You were to follow
the orders I gave,

yet have given orders against me.
Wish-maid
you have been,
yet against my wish you have wished.
Shield-maid
you have been,
yet against me lifted your shield.
Lot-chooser you
were to me,
yet have chosen lots for my downfall.
Hero-carrier
you have been,
yet have stirred up heroes against me.
What once you were,
Wotan has told you.
What now you are,
that tell to yourself!
Wish-maid are you no more;
Valkyrie are you no longer.
So be henceforth
the thing you are now!

BRUNNHILDA.
(violently agitated)

Then you cast me off?
Is that what you mean?

WOTAN.

No more shall I send you from Valhall,
no more shall you call
heroes to death;
no more bring the victors
to fill my hall.
When the gods enjoy the banquet
no more will you proffer
drink from the horn.
No more shall I kiss
the mouth of my child.
Our heavenly host
knows you no longer.
You are cut off

from the race of the gods.
Our ties are broken today,
and from my presence you're banished
    for good.

THE VALKYRIES.

Sorrow! Sorrow!
Sister! Ah, Sister!

BRUNNHILDA.

Must you take all things
that once you gave?

WOTAN.

You must lose all to your lord.
Right here on this rock
punishment starts.
For now you must lie
guardless in sleep.
Whoever happens this way,
and awakes you may take what he finds.

THE VALKYRIES.

Call off, O, father,
call off the curse!
Shall the maiden pale
and be withered by man?
Ah, bring not on her
this crying shame,
Give ear to us,
terrible god!
As her sisters Brunnhild's disgrace is our
    own.

WOTAN.

Have you not heard
what I've decreed?
Your faithless sister
is banished forever from Valhall.
No more with you
will she ride through the air on her
    charger.
Her maidenly flower will fade away.
A husband will gain

all her womanly grace.
She'll have as her master
a masterful man.
She'll sit and spin by the hearth,
as a butt and a mock for scorn.
(Brunnhilda, with a cry, sinks to the ground.
The Valkyries are terrified.)
Fear you her fate?
Then flee from the lost one!
She's to avoid,
so keep from her far!
If one should venture
lingering near her,
holding with her
and defying my will,
the fool will share in her fate:
I warn those who might be bold!
Up and away!
Keep from this mountain!
Haste away as I bid you,
lest bad luck light on you here!

THE VALKYRIES.
(dispersing with a wild cry)
Woe! Woe!
(They are heard riding away at a furious
gallop. The storm gradually abates, the clouds
disperse, evening twilight and then night fall
amid tranquil weather.)

BRUNNHILDA.

Is it so shameful,
what I have done,
that my offense should be punished with
such shame?
Is it so sinful,
what I have done,
that you so harshly should punish that
sin?
Is it so frightful,
what I have done,

that my misdeed should deprive me of
    grace?
O, speak, Father,
look at me frankly.
Silence your rage!
Soften your wrath!
and say to me plain
the guilt so dark
that compels your stubborn despite
thus to cast off your favorite child!

WOTAN.

Ask of your deed!
It plainly tells you your guilt.

BRUNNHILDA.

Yet I obeyed
all your command.

WOTAN.

But did I say
you should fight for the Volsung?

BRUNNHILDA.

As lord of the war
you gave me that word.

WOTAN.

Yet I revoked the
order given amiss.

BRUNNHILDA.

When Fricka had made you
change your intention,
then you were strange to your thinking,
and a foe to yourself.

WOTAN.
(bitterly)

I believe you understand me,
so punished your cunning revolt.
You thought me, though,
craven and fool.
and had I not treason to punish
you would be too slight for my wrath.

BRUNNHILDA.

I'm not too wise, yet

there's one thing I *do* know:
you had love for the Volsung.
I knew of the strife that
rent your mind
and made your heart so forgetful.
You saw a harsh
alternative woe—
a most bitter thought
paining your heart:
that Siegmund should not be shielded.

WOTAN.

You knew this was so,
and yet you gave him your aid?

BRUNNHILDA.

With your weal in mind
I held fast to one thing;
while, in thrall to another,
torn in your thoughts,
helpless, you turned from the problem.
She who kept the rear guard
for Wotan in war,
quite clearly witnessed
what you did not—
Siegmund I beheld.
I faced him,
telling his doom,
encountered his eyes,
gave ear to his words.
I perceived the hero's
sacred distress.
Sad were the sounds
of his manly lamentings—
passionate outcries,
fearful distress,
sadness of spirit,
dauntless disdain.
And my eyes observed,
my ears perceived

that which made me tremble at heart,
in holy, wondering fear.
Shy and stunned,
I stood there in shame.
All I could think of,
how I might serve him,
sharing his fate
in victory or downfall.
What was there other
than this I could choose?
Since he had bred
this love within my heart,
this will that held
the Volsung in my heart,
I trusted his heart,
therefore flaunted his word.

WOTAN.

You did the deed
that I longed to do by myself,
but which twofold need
would not let me perform.
You thought joys of the heart
were so easy to come by,
when burning woe
put my heart in pain,
when terrible need
begat my wrath,
and provoked my wish,
for the world's dear sake,
to enchain my love in my bosom.
When, turning my anger
against my own self, I
arose wroth from my
helpless affliction,
then a most frightful,
urgent desire
impelled me to further my doom
and to bring to an end my woe
with the world I once had created.

You joyed in sweet
and blissful delight,
sensing your rapture,
drunken with joy.
You drank down, smiling,
the drink of love—
while I drink of a drink
mixed of misfortune and gall.
Let your frivolous thoughts
guide you hereafter.
At last you are free from me!
Now I must shun you,
No more may I share
with you my secret counsels.
No more we'll ever labor together.
Nor ever while you live
may the god encounter or greet you.

BRUNNHILDA.

What use was the
foolish maid to you,
who, dazed by your counsel,
misunderstands,
for to me, one counsel
alone could make sense—
to love that which you have loved.
Must I then leave you,
and henceforth shun you?
Must you sever
what once was as one,
abandon half of
what is your being—
that once belonged to you only.
O, god, forget not that!
You'll not dishonor
what is eternal,
seeking a shame that
involves yourself.
You just injure your honor
making me mock for your scorn.

WOTAN.

> You gaily followed
> the power of love:
> follow henceforth
> him whom you must love!

BRUNNHILDA.

> If I depart from Valhall,
> no more with you working and ruling,
> obedient henceforth
> to man and his might,
> then let no craven
> braggart come by;
> let whoso wins be
> a man of worth.

WOTAN.

> You've cut yourself off from me.
> I may not choose him for you.

BRUNNHILDA.

> You brought forth a valorous race;
> no coward could spring from such lineage.
> A hero most high—I know it—
> will bloom from Volsungen blood.

WOTAN.

> Speak not of Volsungen blood!
> From them I parted,
> parting with you.
> Their spite was cause of their doom.

BRUNNHILDA.

> She who turned from you
> rescued their race.
> Sieglinda bears
> the glorious fruit.
> In pain and woe
> Such as no wife has suffered,
> soon she will bear
> what she hides in fear.

WOTAN.

> Don't seek or expect
> help for the bride,
> nor for her fruit to come.

BRUNNHILDA.

> She's saving the sword
> that you made for Siegmund.

WOTAN.

> And for him broke in pieces too.
> Don't strive, O, maid,
> to stir up my spirit!
> But wait for your lot,
> be what it will.
> I cannot choose it for you!
> Yet now I must fare
> forth on my way.
> I've dallied with you too long.
> So I turn from you
> as you have from me.
> I dare not know
> the thing that you wish.
> But this must come:
> the meed due for crime.

BRUNNHILDA.

> What is your intent
> that I must suffer?

WOTAN.

> A heavy sleep
> must lock your eyes.
> He who awakens the maid
> may make her wife, in reward.

BRUNNHILDA.
(falling on her knees)

> Lest fetters of sleep
> firmly bind me,
> as easy booty
> for any coward,
> this one boon must you allow me,
> which holy anguish implores!
> Put frightening horrors
> around me while sleeping,
> that only one who's
> fearless and free
> surely may find me,

on this rock.

WOTAN.

Too much is wanted,
too great a boon.

BRUNNHILDA.
(clinging to his knees)

This one thing must
you allow me!
O, shatter your child
who now clasps your knees;
destroy the dear one,
and crush her to bits;
let your spear put out
the spark of her life;
but give, cruel one, not
such monstrous disgrace as this!
At your command
let fire be kindled.
Let blazing barriers
girdle the rock
to lick with their tongues
and tear with their teeth
the coward who rashly ventures to
come near to the terrible rock!

WOTAN.
(gazes at her in emotion, as he helps her to rise)

Farewell, you valiant,
glorious child!
You, of my heart's most
sanctified pride.
Farewell! farewell! farewell!
Now I must leave you,
and no more greet you
with love and affection.
Nevermore shall you
ride out beside me,
nor hand me mead at meal hour.
Now must I lose you,
you, whom I love so!
O, radiant light in my darkness,

so blazing a fire
shall show your bridal
as never has burned for a bride.
Flickering flames
shall girdle the rock;
The terrible fire
will frighten the cowards.
The weak will flee
from Brunnhilda's rock—
yet one alone masters the bride,
one freer than I, the god!

(*Overcome with joy, Brunnhilda throws herself into his arms.*)

Your bright and glorious eyes,
that I have often caressed,
when lust for war
was paid with kisses,
when heroes' praises
in childish lisp
were sung from loveliest lips—
these most wondrous, radiant eyes,
that lit my way in the storm,
when hopes and longings
had torn my bosom,
when, with a trembling
and wild emotion
I sought sensual pleasures—
I take this last
joy of my life
in this brief and final
farewell kiss!
A luckier man
will joy in your stars.
On me, hapless eternal,
must you close them forever.
For thus turns
the god from his soul,
so kisses your godhood away.
(*He kisses her on both eyes, which at once*

*close. She sinks gently unconscious back in
his arms. He bears her tenderly to a low
mossy bank, shaded by a great fir tree. Again
he gazes on her features, then closes her
helmet visor. Once more he looks sorrowfully
on her form, which he at last covers with the
Valkyrie's steel shield. Then he stalks with
solemn determination to the center of the
stage and turns the point of his spear toward
a mighty rock.)*

Loge, hear!
Hark to me here,
as when first you were found
a fiery flame,
as when first you escaped me,
a wandering fire:
as you were bound,
be so again!
Arise, wavering fire,
surround this rock! Ring it with fire!
Loge! Loge! Arise!
*(At the last invocation he strikes his spear-
point three times against the rock, whereupon
a flame leaps up. It quickly grows to a sea
of flame, which Wotan, with a sign of his
spear, directs to encircle the rock.)*
He who has fear
of Wotan's spear-point
shall never step through the fire!
(He disappears amidst the flames.)

THE END

SIEGFRIED

CHARACTERS

SIEGFRIED

MIME

THE WANDERER *(Wotan)*

ALBERICH

FAFNER

ERDA

FOREST BIRD

BRUNNHILDA

SIEGFRIED

ACT ONE

FIRST SCENE

A Forest

*In the foreground is a portion of a rocky cave. Left, against
the wall stands a large smith's forge, naturally formed of stones,
the bellows alone being artificial. The rough chimney leads up
through the top of the cave. A very large anvil and other smith's
appliances are evident.*

MIME.
*(sitting at the anvil, hammering, with increasing lack of heart,
at a sword. At last, despairful, he stops.)*

>Wearisome torment!
>Meaningless toil!
>I never forged
>a mightier sword:
>though a giant gripped it,
>still it would hold.
>But insolent Siegfried,
>the boy it was made for,
>just whacks and snaps it in two,
>as though 'twere only a toy!
>*(Mime throws the sword angrily on the anvil,
>sets his arms akimbo, and gazes meditatively
>on the ground.)*

157

I know a sword
that he could not shatter:
Needful's fragments
would laugh at his strength
if I could put the pieces together.
But all my skill
cannot forge the sword!
If I could weld the weapon,
I'd be paid in full for my pains!
Fafner, my dragon foe,
lodges within these woods.
He is watching the Nibelung's hoard.
His terrible bulk
guards the gold well.
Siegfried's vigorous strength
may bring about Fafner's end.
The Nibelung's ring
would then be my own.
I know one sword for the deed.
There is a blade that will serve,
if Siegfried grips it in hand.
And I cannot forge it—
Needful the sword!
(He picks up the sword again and resumes
hammering, in deepest dejection.)
Wearisome torment!
Meaningless toil!
I never forged
a mightier sword.
But still its strength
is too weak for the deed!
I tinker and hammer
only because he demands.
He whacks and snaps it in two,
and scolds me, if I don't work!
(He lets the hammer fall.)

SIEGFRIED.
(outside)

Hoi-ho!

(He enters, in a rough forester's dress, with a silver horn hanging by a chain, and boister- ously leading a large bear by a bast rope. In wanton merriment he drives the bear toward Mime.)

Hoi-ho!
come on! come on!
Tear him! tear him, the booby smith!
(Mime drops the sword in terror and flees behind the forge.)
Ha ha ha ha ha ha ha ha ha ha ha ha ha ha ha ha!
(Siegfried drives the bear everywhere after him.)

MIME.

Take him away!
I don't want a bear!

SIEGFRIED.

I come double,
the better to pinch you!
Bruin, ask for the sword!

MIME.

Hey! Put him out!
There lies the weapon.
See, I forged it today.

SIEGFRIED.

Why, for today then, you're free!
(He looses the bear from the rope and gives him a stroke on the back with it.)
Run, Bruin,
I need you no more.
(The bear runs back to the woods; Mime comes trembling from behind the forge.)

MIME.

I've no objection
when you kill them,
but why d'you bring me
your bears alive?

SIEGFRIED.
(sitting down to recover from his laughter)
For want of a better comrade

than the one who sits at home,
I blew my horn in the deep woods,
and waited for an answer,
in the hope that perhaps I would find
a faithful friend,
I asked for one with my horn.
Then a bear broke through the woods,
who growled as he came to me;
and I liked him better than you.
But I'll find better than that!
Then I tied him fast
with rope I had made,
to urge you, old wretch, for the weapon.
(Mime picks up the sword and extends it to
Siegfried.)

MIME.

I made the weapon sharp,
and its edge will gladden your heart.
(He holds the sword timidly in his hand;
Siegfried grabs it from him.)

SIEGFRIED.

What good are its cutting edges
if the steel's not hard and true?
(He tests the sword.)
Hey! what a useless toy is this!
You call this paltry pin a sword?
(He strikes it on the anvil and the pieces fly
in all directions. Mime shrinks with fear.)
And now take the pieces,
blustering bungler!
Would that the blade
had broken your brain-pan!
Why should I let you
cheat any longer,
prating of giants
and wonderful battles,
of deeds of daring,
and dauntless defense?
You'd fashion me weapons,
swords for battle,

praising your art,
proclaiming it good;
yet if I handle
what you have hammered,
a single hand-grip
ruins the trash!
If he were not
so mangy a wretch,
I would pound him to bits
upon his own forge,
the ancient, imbecile imp!
my troubles might then have an end!
(Siegfried in a rage casts himself on a stone
bench. Mime cautiously remains out of his
way.)

MIME.

You rave as though you were mad!
Such gross ingratitude!
If what I try to make
is not done with perfect art,
the graceless, booby boy
forgets to give me thanks!
You always should be grateful.
Remember what I taught you.
You should be willing to listen
to one who loves you so much.
(Siegfried angrily turns his face to the wall,
his back to Mime.)

MIME.

I see you don't want to hear me!
(He stands perplexed, then goes to the
hearth.)
Yet still you'd like some food!
I'll bring the meat that I roasted.
Or would you prefer the soup?
I fixed both just for you.
(He brings the food to Siegfried who, without
turning around, strikes the bowl and meat
from his hand.)

SIEGFRIED.

    Roasts I roast for myself.
    Go and swill your slop alone!

MIME.
(in a wailing voice)

    What a slim reward
    for all my love!
    What a shameful pay
    for my pains!
    A whimpering child
    came to my care.
    You were that babe,
    and I brought you up well,
    gave you warm clothes,
    nourishment too,
    treated you
    just as I did myself.
    And as you grew up
    I waited on you.
    I made you
    a pleasant and restful bed.
    I tinkered your toys
    and a sounding horn;
    toiling for you
    gave me great joy.
    My cunning counsels
    sharpened your wits.
    My shining wisdom
    made you quite bright.
    Here in my home
    I toil and sweat,
    while you roam
    wherever you like.
    I fret and I worry,
    and only for you.
    I wear myself out,
    a poor old dwarf!
    And all I get
    for my worry is this:

that the petulant boy
gives me scorn and hate.

(He sobs.)

*(Siegfried again studies Mime's face. Mime
meets his look and tries to hide the fear in
his own.)*

SIEGFRIED

Mime, I have learned plenty:
you taught me much that I know.
But what you would most like to teach me
is something I cannot learn:
how to endure your sight.
When you bring food and drink to me
         here,
I feel as though I would gag.
When you prepare
a bed for my rest,
I find it harder to sleep.
When you would teach me
how to be wise,
then I would be a fool.
What do I need
but to look at you,
to know you are evil
in all that you do.
I see you stand,
slither and slide,
crawling and slinking,
with your eyelids blinking.
I could take you
by the throat and choke you!
You loathsome wretch,
I could kill you outright!
That's how I love you, my Mime.
If you are clever,
then tell me something,
that long I have sought in vain:
in the woods roaming,

seeking to shun you,
what is it that makes me come back?
For I like the beasts
more dearly than you:
trees and birds,
and the fish in the brook,
truly I like them
much better than you.
What is it then, that makes me come back?
If you're wise, then tell me this.

MIME.
(attempts to approach him winningly.)

My child, that teaches you
that I lie very close to your heart.

SIEGFRIED.

I cannot even stand you,
and just remember that!
(Mime goes back and sits a distance away,
opposite Siegfried.)

MIME.

Your wildness is guilty there.
You should tame it, naughty boy!
Young ones are always crying,
wanting their parents' nest;
love awakens the longing,
and thus do you long for me.
Just so do you love your Mime.
And you have to love him!
As the mother bird loves the birdling,
when it is in the nest,
and before it can flutter,
so, my child, Mime loves—
your wise, considerate Mime—
he loves you like that!

SIEGFRIED.

Hey, Mime, if you're so clever,
then tell me this in your wisdom!
The birdlings were singing
so sweetly in spring,
and each was calling the other.

You said yourself,
when I wished to know,
that they were wives with their husbands.
They chirped and they chattered,
and never did part;
they builded a nest,
and brooded therein;
and after a time
little fledglings were seen,
and both took care of the brood.
And thus in the bush
lay roe-deer in pairs,
and savage wolves and foxes.
Food was brought
to the lair by the father.
The mother suckled the litter.
And there I really learned of love.
And never since then
have I stolen their whelps.
Where have you now, Mime,
your sweet little wifey,
so I may call her mother?

MIME.
(angrily)

Don't be a fool!
Ah, you are dumb!
D'you think you're a bird or a fox?

SIEGFRIED.

A whimpering child
came to your care,
I was that babe,
and you cared for me well.
But tell me,
where did you find the poor mite?
You didn't do badly
without a wife.

MIME.
(greatly embarrassed)
Just believe

whatever I tell you:
I am your father
and mother combined.

SIEGFRIED.

You lie, contemptible gawk!
For that young ones are like their parents,
I know, for I've seen for myself.
I came to the crystal brook.
There were animals there
and trees reflected.
Thus, were mirrored,
just as they are,
most brightly, the sun and the clouds.
And there in that pool
I saw my form;
it looked to me
quite different from yours.
A glittering fish
is as much like a toad;
and fish can't have toads for their fathers!

MIME.
(*much vexed*)

What a display
of nonsense is this!

SIEGFRIED.

See here, I find
I know at last
what I've sought so often in vain:
when I flee from you
and run to the forest,
do you know why I return?
Because you haven't yet told me
what father and mother are mine.

MIME.

What father? What mother?
Meaningless question!

SIEGFRIED.
(*gripping Mime by the throat*)

Why then I must choke you,
till you can tell me:

good manners are wasted on you!
So I shall have
to make you answer.
If I had not
forced you to teach me,
I would not even
know how to speak!
So out with it,
scabby old fool!
Who are my father and mother?

MIME.
(after making signs with his head and hands, is released by Siegfried.)

You almost choked me to death!
Let go, and I'll say what you want.
I'll tell you all that I know.
O, unthankful
and wicked child!
Now hear and learn why you hate me!
I am no father
or kin of yours;
and yet you should thank me for life!
You owe all to me,
your one only friend;
just my pity alone
lets you stay here.
A lovely payment I get!
I'm a wishful thinker,
a fool!
A poor woman lay weeping,
out in the fearful woods:
I helped her here to this cave,
and let her stay by my hearth-side.
A child lived in her body;
(Sad is the story now.)
The boy was born in woe.
I helped as best I could.
Great was her pain! she died—
but Siegfried saw the day.

SIEGFRIED.

She died so that Siegfried might live?

MIME.

She delivered you to my care:
I gladly took the child.
What love I lavished on you!
What kindness and care I bestowed!
A whimpering child
came to my care.

SIEGFRIED.

I think you have said that before!
Now say just why I'm called Siegfried?

MIME.

Because your dear mother
asked it to be so;
and with that name
you grew strong and fair.
For you were that child
and I brought you up well.

SIEGFRIED.

Now tell me the name of my mother.

MIME.

I hardly know her name!
Gave you warm clothes,
nourishment too—

SIEGFRIED.

Her name has not yet been told me!

MIME.

I don't think I know. But wait!
Sieglinda—there, now I have it!
In grief she gave you to me.
I treated you just as I did myself—

SIEGFRIED.

Then tell me, who was my father?

MIME.

I never saw his face.

SIEGFRIED.

But my mother spoke of my father?

MIME.

He fell in battle,

was all that she said;
she left you, fatherless,
here in my care.
And as you grew up,
I waited on you,
and made you
a pleasant and restful bed—

SIEGFRIED.

Always the same old
starling song!
If I may but believe you,
if you are speaking truly,
then let me see some proof!

MIME.

What proof then shall I show you?

SIEGFRIED.

My ears can give you no trust,
I trust you but with my eyes;
what witness can you show?

MIME.
*(After some thought he fetches the two pieces of a broken
sword.)*

This once your mother gave me.
For lodging, food and service,
this was my slender pay.
See here, just a broken sword!
She said your father had borne this
in the fight in which he was slain.

SIEGFRIED.
(enthusiastically)

And you shall weld
these pieces together:
I'll swing then my rightful sword!
Up! hurry up, Mime!
Waste no more time!
What can you do?
Now show me your skill!
Fool me no more
with worthless trash!
The faith that I have

lies in this sword!
If there's a flaw
seen in your work,
if you can't fashion
this trusty steel,
then, coward, look to your skin,
for I shall polish it well!
This day, I swear
I shall handle the sword.
This weapon today shall be mine!

MIME.

But why do you want it today?

SIEGFRIED.

I shall wander
from this forest, nevermore to return!
I am free
and I am happy.
Nothing binds me to you,
for I am not your son.
I shall find a home afar!
Your hearth is not my house,
nor your roof my shelter now!
As the fish
sports in the water,
as the finch
wings through the heavens,
So too shall I
fly far away,
like the wind when it whistles
through the woods.
So, Mime, I leave you for good.
(He runs into the forest.)

MIME.

Hey there! Hey there! Siegfried! Come
back!
Hey! Siegfried! Siegfried! Hey!
*(For a while he looks in the direction of
Siegfried, stunned. Then he returns to his
smithy, and seats himself behind the anvil.)*

He storms away!
And here I sit!
Old cares are gone;
now I have new ones.
I'm baffled, caught and nailed down!
Now what shall I do?
How keep him in tow?
How lead this young madman
to Fafner's lair?
And how forge the fragments
of obstinate steel?
There's no furnace fire
able to fuse them,
nor can dwarf-held hammer
conquer their hardness.
The Nibelung's hate,
toil and sweat,
cannot make Needful new!
All I have done—is in vain!

(He sobs.)

SECOND SCENE

Wanderer (Wotan) steps out of the woods to the back entrance of the cave. He is wearing a long dark blue cloak and bearing a spear as a staff. On his head is a round, drooping broad-brimmed hat.

Hail there, cunning smith!
A way-weary guest looks for shelter
at your hearth!

MIME.

What's this?
Who are you
that come to this wild
and that seek me in woodland wastes?

WANDERER.

"Wanderer"—so I am called,
much travel I've seen.
I have wandered far and wide
on this earth.

MIME.

Then wander some more.
Just be on your way
if you wander the world!

WANDERER.

Good men always receive me;
many even offer gifts.
Unhandsome is
as unhandsome does.

MIME.

Ill luck always
lived in my home.
Why do you want to increase it?

173

WANDERER.
(constantly and slowly stepping nearer)

> Much I've sought for
> and much I've learned.
> I have made men
> wise and knowing,
> saving many
> from their sorrows,
> healing their wounded hearts.

MIME.

> Wisdom is yours,
> you have found a great deal,
> but here I don't need any teacher.
> I am lonely,
> and lone would be,
> loiterers cannot stay here.

WANDERER.

> Many fancy
> wisdom is theirs,
> yet most of all lack
> what they most need.
> When they ask me,
> seeking for knowledge,
> then I teach them my lore.

MIME.
(more and more anxious as he sees the Wanderer approach.)

> Many cherish
> worthless wisdom,
> but I have knowledge enough
> and my wits are good,
> I want ńo more!
> So, wise one, be on your way!

WANDERER.
(sitting down at the hearth)

> I'll sit by the hearth,
> and wager my head.
> We'll have a battle of wits.
> My head is yours,
> you take it at will,
> as pledge when you ask,

if you learn
knowledge you cannot find good.

MIME.
(who has been staring at the Wanderer open-mouthed, now shrinks back.)

How shall I get out of this trap?
I'll ask him something quite tricky.

(aloud)

Your head wagered
for my hearth.
Be wise and careful to keep it!
Thrice I freely
ask what I will!

WANDERER.

Three times must I hit it.

MIME.
(sets himself to meditation)

You've roamed a great deal
on the world's broad surface,
you've wandered much on the earth.
So show me your skill.
What is the race
dwelling beneath earth's surface?

WANDERER.

Why, the dusky Nibelungs
people the rocky caverns:
Nibelhome is their land.
Black elves, those Nibelungs.
Black Alberich
mastered their might by a spell!
By a magic ring
a powerful charm
tamed this industrious folk;
wondrous treasures,
shimmering bright,
fell then to him.
With these could the world be his
kingdom.
Now ask me your second point.

MIME.

(sinks in continually deeper meditation)

> Yes, Wanderer,
> much you know
> of the central caves of earth.
> Now answer me straight,
> what is the race
> dwelling upon earth's surface?

WANDERER.

> Well, the race of giants
> live on the surface of earth:
> Gianthome is their land.
> Fasolt and Fafner,
> the rowdy rulers,
> envied the Nibelungs' might;
> and they won for themselves
> the powerful hoard;
> and thus the ring fell to them.
> The hoard brought hate,
> and the brothers fought.
> Grim death took Fasolt,
> In dragon's shape
> Fafner now watches the hoard.
> One question more is to come.

MIME.

(absorbed in thought)

> Yes, Wanderer,
> much you know
> of the earth and all its regions.
> Now give me the truth!
> Tell me what race
> dwells on cloud-covered heights?

WANDERER.

> The gods hold the heights,
> dwelling in glory.
> Valhall is their home.
> These gods are light elves;
> Light-Alberich,
> Wotan, rules them as king.
> From the world-ash's

mystical branches
once he fashioned a spear.
Ash trees fade,
but the shaft cannot fail;
and with its spear-point
Wotan rules the world.
Deep in the shaft
he cut his runes,
telling of truth to pacts.
To own the spear
gripped by the god
is to hold sway
like Wotan, over all:
the Nibelung host
must bow to the spear.
The giants as well
call him their lord.
All must obey as their master
the one who holds the spear.
(He strikes the spear, as if by accident, on the
ground. A light thunderclap is heard, which
quite unsettles Mime.)
Now tell me, cunning dwarf,
have I disclosed the truth?
and please may I keep my head?
(Mime, after having attentively watched the
Wanderer with the spear, falls into a state of
terror, confusedly seeks for his tools, and
looks nervously aside.)

MIME.

Keep it—you're free,
safe from my sword!
So, Wanderer, be on your way!

WANDERER.

You should really have asked
something worth knowing,
for I had wagered my head.
Since you know nothing
that you should,
you therefore must wager your own.

You were quite
rude to your guest;
my head stood
as a pledge to you,
to win a place at your hearth.
Now duty's pledge
binds you to me.
Answer me thrice
or forfeit your life.
Be resolute, Mime, and bold!

MIME.
(*finally composing himself*)

I left home
many years ago,
long have parted
from my mother earth.
I feel Wotan's eye upon me,
he spies right into this cave,
his gaze withers
my mother wit.
But now it is wise to be wise,
Wanderer, ask what you will!
Perhaps fortune will help me
to ransom my dwarfish head!

WANDERER.
(*again leisurely seating himself*)

Now, honorable dwarf,
first of the questions.
Tell me, what is the race
that Wotan treats so harshly,
and yet loves most dearly of all?

MIME.
(*more cheerful now*)

Little know I
of heroes' kindred,
but just the same I shall be free.
The Volsungen are
the chosen race
that Wotan cared for
and loved so dearly,

though he was harsh to them:
Siegmund and Sieglinda,
offspring of Volsa,
a wild and desperate
twin-born pair.
Siegfried sprang from their loins,
the strongest Volsung of all.
Now have I, Wanderer,
this once saved my head?

WANDERER.
(pleasantly)

Yes, you have
answered me well, I confess!
Rogues like you are quite skillful.
You answered well
the first point put.
A second comes now, my friend!
A cunning Nibelung
Harbors Siegfried,
Fafner's destined destroyer—
for the boy is to slay him,
to let the dwarf gain the gold.
Name the sword
that Siegfried must handle,
if he's to slay the foe?

MIME.
(feeling much better, now joyfully rubs his hands)

Needful is
the coveted sword,
and Wotan thrust it deep
in an ash tree.
Just one could possess it,
he who could pull it out.
The strongest heroes
tried it in vain;
Siegmund succeeded,
he alone.
Then he bore it to war,
till on Wotan's spear it was split.

Now a cunning smith
has preserved the parts,
for he knows it is only
with Wotan's sword,
a valiant, foolish boy,
Siegfried, shall slay the foe.

(much pleased)

Now may I keep
my head-piece a while?

WANDERER.

Ha ha ha ha, ha ha ha ha!
One wittier I have
never encountered;
for where can your like be found?
But if by your ruse,
the valorous stripling
fulfills your dwarfish intentions,
there's a third and final
threat to come!
Tell me, you cunning weapon-smith,
who shall from the mighty pieces
fashion the sword called Needful?

MIME.
(starts up in extreme terror)

The pieces! the sword!
O woe! I'm dizzy!
How shall I start?
What follows now?
Accursed steel!
Why was it I stole you!
A sword that has pierced me
with want and woe!
Still it remains
too hard for my hammer.
Rivet, solder,
fail in the test!
The cleverest smith's
lacking in skill!
*(As though out of his senses, he flings his tools
about, and breaks out in despair.)*

Who can forge the sword
if I cannot?
How shall I give you an answer?

WANDERER.

Thrice your questions were put me,
thrice the challenge was met.
You sought for knowledge
far afield,
yet failed to ask what you ought.
What would help
was right at hand.
Now when I guess it,
you are upset.
Your witty head
is the prize I have won!
Now, Fafner's dauntless destroyer,
hear, and learn your doom:
"He who has never
harbored fear,
he shall forge the sword."
(Mime stares at him. He turns to depart.)
Guard well your head.
henceforth take care:
I leave it forfeit to him
who has never harbored fear!

*(He turns away with a smile and disappears into the forest.
Mime sinks down into his seat, as if overwhelmed.)*

THIRD SCENE

MIME.
(He is staring into the sunlit forest, and gradually gives way to violent trembling.)

> Accursed light!
> What makes the air flame?
> What flickers and flashes,
> what quivers and whirs,
> what floats there and soars,
> and flickers around?
> It glimmers and gleams
> in the sunlight's glow!
> What rustles and hums
> and whistles so loud?
> It growls and roars
> and crackles this way!
> It breaks through the wood,
> making for me!

> *(He rises up in terror.)*

> Its horrible jaws
> open up wide:
> The dragon will seize me!
> Fafner! Fafner!
> *(He sinks down shrieking behind the anvil as Siegfried breaks through the thicket.)*

SIEGFRIED.

> Hey, there! you slowpoke!
> Are you now ready?

> *(Siegfried enters the cave.)*

183

How much have you done?
(He pauses in surprise.)
Where is the smith?
Where has he hid?
Hey-hey! Mime, you 'fraid-cat!
Where are you? Reveal yourself!

MIME.
(weakly, from behind the anvil)
Is it you, child!
Come you alone?

SIEGFRIED.
(laughing)
Under the anvil?
Say, a nice place to work!
Were you sharpening the sword?

MIME.
(coming forward greatly disturbed and confused)
The sword? The sword?
How could I forget it?
"He who has never
harbored fear,
he shall forge the sword."
I had more sense
than to try such work!

SIEGFRIED.
(vehemently)
Will you now tell me?
or must I teach you?

MIME.
I do not know what to say!
I've lost my head,
lost it by wager,
for henceforth 'tis forfeit to him
"who has never harbored fear."

SIEGFRIED.
Ha! so you flout me?
thinking to flee?

MIME.
(gradually taking hold of himself)
I'd flee the man

who harbors fear!
Fear was the teaching I failed in;
I dumbly forgot
the one good thing.
Love was the lesson
that I gave you;
but alas, the lesson failed!
Now how can I make you feel fear?

SIEGFRIED.
(seizes him)

Hey! must I help you?
What's done for today?

MIME.

While sunk in my thoughts,
considering your welfare,
something important I thought of.

SIEGFRIED.
(laughing)

You mean you were sunk
under the anvil.
However, get on with your tale.

MIME.
(recovering himself more and more)

I learned the meaning of fear,
so I could teach you, blockhead.

SIEGFRIED.

Well, tell me about it.

MIME.

You've never felt fear,
and yet you would leave
these woods for the world?
What good is the trustiest sword,
if you are lacking in fear?

SIEGFRIED.
(impatiently)

Now you give me stupid advice!

MIME.
(approaching Siegfried with increasing confidence)

But your mother's words
sound from my lips;

such was my promise,
so I must keep it:
not to let you fare forth
away from this forest,
until you're acquainted with fear.

SIEGFRIED.
(vehemently,)

If it's an art,
why was I not taught?
Come on! Now tell me what fear is!

MIME.

Have you not felt
in dusky woods,
when twilight falls,
in gloomy glens,
when comes a whisper,
hum and hiss,
when savage sounds approach,
flick'ring flashes
hover round you,
growing growlings
to make you shake—

(trembling)

have you not felt then
grisly horrors take hold of your body,
terrible shudders
set you a-tremble?
Then your heart throbbing within
bursts with terror and fright!
If this is still unknown,
then fear is strange to your heart.

SIEGFRIED.
(meditating)

Curious, surely,
that must be.
Hard and fast
beats my heart in my breast.
The shiv'ring and shaking,
the glowing and quaking
burning and fainting,

throbbing and trembling,
these are much to my liking.
Great is my longing for fear!
But how can you teach it to me?
How could you, coward, instruct me?

MIME.

Merely obey,
I know the way well;
I have figured it out.
I know of a dragon foe,
who kills and eats his fill.
Fafner surely can teach you.
Follow me to where he lives.

SIEGFRIED.

And where is his lair?

MIME.

Hate-cavern,
that is its name;
due east, at end of the wood.

SIEGFRIED.

Then not too far from the world?

MIME.

From Hate-cave the world is not far.

SIEGFRIED.

Then that is where you must lead me:
fear shall be taught me,
then forth to the world!
Be quick! Forge me the sword!
In the world fain would I swing it.

MIME.

The sword? Alack!

SIEGFRIED.

Quick to the smithy!
Show me your work!

MIME.

Accursed steel!
The job is too much for my skill;
no dwarfish power
avails with the magic spell.
There is one for the work,

he who has never felt fear.

SIEGFRIED.

Pleasant tricks
the idler would play me.
Only a bungler,
that's all you are!
You think you can trick me with lies!
Bring me the pieces!
Off with the bungler!
(stepping to the hearth)
My father's steel
yields but to me.
Let me fashion the sword.
(Flinging Mime's tools about, he sets impetu-
ously to work.)

MIME.

If you had labored
to learn your craft,
you now would know what to do;
but you were always
lazy at work:
you see what good this has done you!

SIEGFRIED.

Where the master has failed
could pupil do better,
even if he had obeyed?
Just go away.
Make yourself scarce,
or else I will forge you also!
(He makes a large pile of charcoal on the
hearth and blows the fire, while he screws the
pieces of sword in a vice and files away.)

MIME.
(who has sat down a little away, watches Siegfried at work)
Now what is all this?
There is the solder.
The brew waits for your skill.

SIEGFRIED.

Out on the brew,
I need it not!

I use no pap for my sword!

MIME.

But the file is wearing,
the rasp is ruined!
You're fretting the steel to splinters.

SIEGFRIED.

It must be splintered
and ground into shreds:
what is broken
then can be patched.
                    (He goes on filing energetically.)

MIME.
(aside)

No craftsman helps here,
I see that well.
What helps the booby is folly alone.
How the boy toils,
and moves with might!
The steel is in shreds,
and yet he's not tired!
*(Siegfried has fanned the hearthfire into a
                    very bright glow.)*
Although I'm as old
as cave and wood,
I've never seen such a sight!
*(While Siegfried continues his impetuous
                    filing, Mime seats himself farther off.)*
He will forge the sword,
I know that well.
Lacking fear he will win.
The Wand'rer knew it well.
So how to hide
my hapless head?
It goes to Siegfried unless
Fafner acquaints him with fear.
*(springing up and bending low with growing
                              restlessness)*
My plight is woeful!
If Siegfried learns fear,
then how can he conquer the foe?

And I will still lack the ring.
Accursed dilemma!
What shall I do?
Who can give good advice,
so the valorous boy can be tamed.
(Siegfried has now filed the pieces down and put them in a crucible, which he sets on the fire.)

SIEGFRIED.

Hey Mime! Be quick!
and name the sword
that I have shredded to pieces.

MIME.

Needful, that is
the name of the sword:
for your mother told me the tale.

SIEGFRIED.
(During the following song he blows the fire with the bellows.)

Needful! Needful!
conquering sword!
What mighty blow could break you?
I filed the beautiful blade
to shreds,
and now I'll fry all the filings.
Ho-ho! Ho-ho!
Ho-hei! Ho-hei! Ho-ho!
Bellows blow!
Brighten the glow!
Once I felled
a mighty ash
which grew in the forest glen.
I burnt the tree
until it was coal;
now it lies heaped high on the hearth.
Ho-ho! Ho-ho!
Ho-hei! Ho-hei! Ho-ho!
Bellows blow!
Brighten the glow!
The charcoal pieces—
how fierce they burn!

How bright and fair they glow!
They shoot through the air
in showering sparks,
ho-hei, ho-ho, ho-hei!
Now melt me my filings of steel.
Ho-ho! ho-ho! ho-ho!
Ho-hei! Ho-hei! Ho-ho!
Bellows blow!
Brighten the glow!

MIME.
(still by himself, sitting at a distance)

He'll finish the sword
and finish Fafner;
that's easy enough to foresee.
Hoard and ring
will fall to his hands.
So just how shall I win the prize?
                (A sudden thought comes to Mime.)
By hook or crook
I'll win both prizes
and save my head besides.

SIEGFRIED.
(again at the bellows)

Ho-ho! Ho-ho!
Ho-ho, ho-hei! Ho-hei!

MIME.

After his fight he'll be tired;
a drink should be to his taste.
I've spicy simples,
recently gathered;
these I will brew for him.
All he needs is a drop
of this potion—
senseless then he will lie.
With the very weapon
that now he is forging,
he shall be cleared from my way,
then hoard and the ring are mine.

SIEGFRIED.

Needful! Needful!

Sword that I need!
At last all your filings melt,
and now you swim
amid your sweat.

MIME.

(He rubs his hands with delight.)

Hey, clever Wanderer!
Was I so dumb?
Don't you think I have
a pretty wit?
Is not this
the simplest way?

SIEGFRIED.

(He pours the glowing contents of the crucible into a mold and holds it on high.)

I'll soon be swinging my sword!
(He plunges the mold into the pail of water.
Steam and hissing ensue.)

In the water flowed
a flood of fire;
furious hate
hissed from its waves!
But though it flowed hot
in the watery flood,
now does it rest.
There, see how it lies,
proud in its lordly strength.
Blood will drip soon,
bathing the blade.
(He thrusts the steel into the fire and works
the bellows violently. Mime springs up,
happy; he fetches several vessels, shakes from
them spices and herbs into a cooking pot.)
Now sweat once again,
and then I can forge you!
Needful, sword that I need!
(During his work he observes Mime who is
carefully placing the pot on the fire.)
Hey, stupid!
What's that mess on the fire?

While I burn steel
what is it you brew?

MIME.

A smith has come to shame:
a boy can now teach him skill;
for the poor old man has lost his art,
and so becomes a cook.
Burn all your iron to broth,
while I prepare you
soup with nice eggs.

(He goes on cooking.)

SIEGFRIED.

Mime, the artist,
takes up cooking,
because he's tired of his forge.
I have shattered
all his swords into pieces.
I refuse to eat what he cooks!
*(During the following Siegfried draws the
mold from the fire, breaks it open and lays
the glowing steel on the anvil.)*
He'd teach me the meaning
of fear and danger!
I don't want him for a teacher,
for the best he can do
is take up my time.
He's only a foolish old bungler!
Ho-ho! Ho-ho! Ho-hei!
Hammering blows make you strong and
hard!
Ho-ho! Ha-hei! Hoho! Ha-hei!
Hot blood once stained
your steely blue;
its ruddy trickling
reddened your blade.
Cold then was your laugh;
you licked the blade till it cooled.
Hei-a-ho! Ha-ha! Ha-hei-a-ha!
The fiery flame
now makes you glow,

while my hammer pounds
on your pliant steel.
Now you're tame you are angry,
and spray me fiercely with sparks.
Hei-a-ho! Hei-a-ho!
Hei-a-ho-ho-ho-ho-ho!
Ha-hei! Hahei! Ha-hei!

MIME.

He's making a sharp-edged sword,
that's to kill Fafner
the Nibelungs' foe.
I've brewed a poisoned drink;
Siegfried will take it
when Fafner falls.
My wits must gain me the prize.
Fortune smiles on the wise.

SIEGFRIED.

Ho-ho! Ho-ho! Ho-ho! Ho-hei!
Hammering blows
make you strong and hard!
Ho-ho! Ha-hei!
Ho-ho! Ha-hei!
The merry sparks
make me laugh with joy!
The brave look fairer
when fired by wrath.
Lo! you're laughing at me,
yet you look grisly and grim!
Hei-a-ho, ha-ha, ha-hei-a-ha!
The heat and hammer
serve me well.
I beat you out
with sturdy strokes.
Now banish your ruddy shame,
and be as cold and hard as you can.
Hei-a-ho! Hei-a-ho!
Hei-a-ho-ho-ho-ho-ho! Hei-ah!
*(He swings the blade and plunges it into the
pail of water, then laughs aloud at the hiss-
ing.)*

MIME.

Once my brother
made a shimmering ring,
infusing a spell
of magical might.
Its shining gold
can give pow'r to men,
pow'r more than is dreamed of!
This pow'r is mine!
Alberich, you
whom once I served,
shall in your turn
be servant to me,
and down I'll descend,
Nibelungs' leader,
and all his host
shall call me lord.
The contemptible dwarf
shall now be obeyed!
For they love the gold,
gods and heroes both.
The world shall henceforth
bow to my nod,
and at my anger
tremble with fear.

SIEGFRIED.

Needful! Needful!
Conquering sword!
You rest again, fast in your hilt!

MIME.

Why then my toil
is finished and done.

SIEGFRIED.

You were in two,
but now you are one.
No blow shall evermore destroy you.

MIME.

Let others win for me
endless wealth.

SIEGFRIED.

The dying father
destroyed the steel,
the living son
forged it anew.
The blade gives a ringing laugh,
and its keenness cuts with a will!

MIME.

Mime, the valiant,
Mime, is master,
Prince of Nibelungs,
lord of the World!

SIEGFRIED.

Needful! Needful!
Conquering sword!
Again I've waked you to life.
Once you lay
in lifeless bits,
but now you shine
proud in your strength.

MIME.

Hey, Mime, how lucky you are!

SIEGFRIED.

Just let the villains
see how you shine!

MIME.

Could any have dreamed of this?

SIEGFRIED.

Slash at the rascal,
cut down the rogue!
See, Mime, you smith,
see how my sword can cleave!

(He strikes the anvil, which splits asunder with a mighty noise. Mime, who has jumped joyfully on a stool, falls terrified to the ground. Siegfried, exultant, holds the sword aloft.)

ACT TWO

FIRST SCENE

Night, in a deep forest. In the far background the entrance to a cave. To the left a fissured cliff is seen through the trees.

The dwarf Alberich is lying by the rocky cliff, brooding gloomily.

ALBERICH.

Within this wood
I watch at Fafner's cave;
I prick my ear,
peering through the gloom.
Fateful day,
have you arrived?
Are you the dawn
on the heels of night?
(In the wood, from the right, a storm arises;
a bluish light shines thence.)
What is the gleam glimmering there?
Nearby shimmers
a shining light;
it runs like a fiery steed,
breaks through the wood,
rushing this way!

Is it the dragon-slayer?
Is Fafner's doom so near?
The light goes out,
The glow hides from my sight.
Night is master.
*(The Wanderer enters from the wood and
                    stops, facing Alberich.)*
Who comes here, shining through
        shadows?

WANDERER.

I come
to your hate-cave by night.
Who confronts me within the dark?
*(The moonlight breaks forth and lights up the
                    Wanderer's figure.)*

ALBERICH.

So you dare to come here?
What would you then?
Out of the way!
Go elsewhere, shameless thief!

WANDERER.
(quietly)

Black Alberich!
Is it you
guarding old Fafner's house?

ALBERICH.

What are you seeking?
More evil deeds?
Wander away!
Take yourself elsewhere!
You've drenched the place
with evil deception enough!
Therefore, bounder,
take yourself off!

WANDERER.

I came as watcher, not as plotter.
Who hinders the Wanderer's way?

ALBERICH.

You vile, villainous trickster!
Were I still the fool

that I was for your sake,
the time I let you bind me,
the ring would not
be my own much longer, I warrant!
Take care; for I know
all of your tricks!
I see your weakness—
that is clear to my vision.
You paid as debtor
using my treasure;
my ring paid for
the giants' toil;
your castle grew by their work.
What you did promise once to the
    bullies,
in words engraved in runes
on the lordly shaft of your spear,
you dare not
contradict by your might,
by seizing wages they worked for;
or else you yourself
would cause your spear to split;
within your hand
your wonderful staff,
so mighty, would shiver to bits.

WANDERER.

But its runes of truth to treaties
wretch, did not
bind you to me.
Instead it bends your will to mine:
I guard it well in the war.

ALBERICH.

You proudly boast
of marvelous power,
yet there is fear in your heart!
My curse has foredoomed
to death
the guard of the golden treasure.
Then—whom will it fall to?

Will the coveted hoard
belong again to the Nibelung?
That gnaws you with endless worry!
For just let it come
again to my hand,
not like the stupid giants
will I employ its power:
then tremble, you ageless
helper of heroes!
I will conquer
Valhall with Hella's host!
The world then shall be mine!

WANDERER.

I know well
what you mean,
but care not at all;
whoever wins it,
let him be lord.

ALBERICH.

You tell me darkly
what already is known!
On heroes' children
pin all your pride,
those dears who have bloomed from your
blood!
Have you not fostered a youngling
to pick the fruit you hope for
but dare not pluck yourself?

WANDERER.

Don't taunt me:
quarrel with Mime;
he brings you danger and woe.
He is coming here with a boy.
The lad will lay Fafner low.
I'm not known to him,
the Nibelung makes him his tool.
So let me say, my friend,
freely do what you will!

(Alberich makes a violent move of curiosity.)

Mark my words well!
Be on your guard!
He does not know of the ring,
but Mime soon will explain.

ALBERICH.

Will the hoard stay untouched by you?

WANDERER.

Those I favor
work out their own salvation.
He stands or he falls,
his own right lord;
heroes, though, help to my purpose.

ALBERICH.

Is none but Mime
my rival in this?

WANDERER.

Only he, beside you,
covets the gold.

ALBERICH.

And so shall I make it my own?

WANDERER.

A hero nears
to rescue the hoard;
two Nibelungs covet the gold.
Fafner falls,
he who guards the ring.
After that, finders are keepers.
Would you know more?
There lies the foe.
If you warn him of death,
maybe he'll give you the toy.
So now I'll wake him for you.
Fafner! Fafner!
O, Fafner, wake!

ALBERICH.
(astonished)

What's the madman doing?
Mine is it really?

FAFNER'S VOICE.

Who stirs me from sleep?

WANDERER.
(facing cave)

A friend has arrived,
to warn you of danger—
if you will make return
of the treasure you are guarding.
(He bends his ear toward the cave, listening.)

FAFNER'S VOICE.

What would he?

ALBERICH.
(has stepped toward the Wanderer and calls into the cave.)

Waken, Fafner!
Dragon, awake!
A mighty hero nears!
He means to send you to heaven!

FAFNER'S VOICE.

My stomach hears.

WANDERER.

Bold is the boy, and strong,
keen-cutting his sword.

ALBERICH.

He craves the ring,
nothing but that.
Leave it to me as pay:
no fight will take place.
Your hoard will be safe,
and long you'll live in peace.

FAFNER'S VOICE.

I have, and I hold!
Let me slumber!

WANDERER.
(He laughs aloud, then turns again to Alberich.)

Well, Alberich, that trick failed.
Yet call me rogue no more!
I give you counsel,
listen to this:
all things go their wonted way,
think not fate can be altered.
I leave you alone here,
hold yourself firm!

Contend with Mime, your brother;
for his kind, I think, suits you better.

(turning to go)

The other things
you'll quickly find out!
*(He vanishes into the wood. A storm arises, a
bright glow breaks out, then both quickly
cease. Alberich's eyes follow the Wanderer.)*

ALBERICH.

He's riding away.
His steed is fast.
He leaves me in care and shame.
Yet laugh away,
you light-spirited,
luxurious
gang of eternals!
One day
I shall see you all die!
The wise one keeps
a patient watch,
while the gold brightly gleams.
Hatred dogs you, beware!
*(He slips into the cleft. The stage remains empty. Morning
twilight.)*

SECOND SCENE

As day breaks Siegfried and Mime enter. Siegfried is bearing a sword hung in a girdle of rope. Mime carefully examines the place.

MIME.

We go no farther!
Stay right here!

SIEGFRIED.
(sits down under a lime tree and looks round him)

Here then shall I learn the lesson?
Far have your footsteps led me.
We have wandered through this forest
a live-long, wearisome night.
Mime, I want you
to leave me!
Either I learn
what I ought to here,
or else I shall go elsewhere—
then I'll be finally free!

MIME.

Truly, dear one,
if today
and here you seek in vain,
no other place,
no other time,
ever will serve as well.

See it there,
the gloomy cavern mouth?
Therein dwells
a fearful dragon foe;
terribly cruel
is he, and huge;
his horrible jaws
can open up wide,
and with a gulp
the wicked brute will gladly swallow **you**
      whole.

SIEGFRIED.

Good then, to close up his gullet;
he'll not take a bite out of me.

MIME.

Venom pours
from his slavering mouth;
if but a drop
should spatter on you,
your flesh and your bones would wilt.

SIEGFRIED.

I will step aside as I fight him,
letting no poison come near.

MIME.

His serpent tail
lashes about,
and should it seize you fast
and squeeze you tight,
your limbs would be broken like glass!

SIEGFRIED.

I will guard myself from this twister,
keeping the monster in sight.
But answer me this:
has the brute a heart?

MIME.

A terrible, cruel heart.

SIEGFRIED.

And does it lie
in the normal place,

as in men or in beasts?

MIME.

Of course, young one,
exactly like theirs—
and now do you feel any fear?

SIEGFRIED.
(suddenly sitting up)

Needful, pierce
the proud heart of the brute!
Is this like the fear you speak of?
Hey! You dotard!
Where's your cunning?
Can you not
teach me any more?
Go on your way then farther:
I cannot learn my fear here.

MIME.

Wait just a bit!
You think I utter
nothing but empty sound;
have patience, hear and
see for yourself,
and then you will faint in your fear.
When your vision swims,
and footing grows weak,
your heart will pound
your breast in fear;
then thank the one who has led you,
and think how great is my love.

SIEGFRIED.

Your love is not welcome!
Did I not say,
out of my sight for good!
Leave me alone,
I want no more talk about love,
that I can stomach no more!
That sickening nodding,
and eyelids blinking
I'm sick and tired
of such a sight!

When shall I be free from the fool?

MIME.

I leave you now,
I'll lie down at the spring.
Stay in this place;
then, when the sun has come up,
look for your foe.
You will see him slither this way,
heading here
from the cave.
He seeks this stream when thirsty.

SIEGFRIED.
(laughing)

Mime, wait at the spring,
and there I'll let him safely go.
First I'll wait
till I see he is drinking,
then with my sword
I will stab his kidneys.
So now hear my advice:
do not rest near the spring;
go somewhere else,
much farther off,
and stay away for good!

MIME.

The terrible fight
may quite exhaust you,
then you may find me helpful.
(Siegfried turns away violently.)
Call for your friend
if you crave counsel,
or if fear comes to beat at your heart.
*(Siegfried rises and drives Mime away with
furious gestures.)*
Fafner and Siegfried,
Siegfried and Fafner,
Oh! slay each other, you two!
*(He disappears in the woods. Siegfried
stretches out comfortably under the lime
tree and watches the departing Mime.)*

SIEGFRIED.

My heart is throbbing with joy!
I know I am not his son!
Never before
was the wood so fresh;
never day
had so lovely a laugh,
since the rascally wretch has gone,
never more to confront my sight.
                    (*He falls into silent meditation.*)
How did my father look?
Ha! indeed, like myself!
For would not the son of a dwarf
look like a dwarf,
just like Mime?
Even as loathsome,
grizzled and gray,
small and wry,
humpbacked and hobbling,
with ears that are hanging,
eyes that are bleary?
Off with the imp!
I hope he's gone for good!
(*He leans farther back and looks up through
the branches. Deep silence. Forest murmurs.*)
I wish I knew
what my mother was like!
But thoughts cannot
show me her picture!

(*very tenderly*)

Her eyes must have shone,
shimmering bright,
like the eyes of a roe-deer,
only more lovely!

(*very softly*)

She bore me when in anguish,
but why did she die through me?
Must then all human mothers
die when their children
come to the world?

Sad the world would be, faith!
Ah, might the son
only see his mother!
Lovely—mother,
who lived on earth!
(*He sighs softly and leans still farther back.
Deep silence. Growing forest murmurs. At
length Siegfried's attention is caught by the
song of the wood bird. He listens with growing interest to the sounds coming from the
branches above him.*)

You gracious birdling,
your song is so strange!
Say, is this forest your home?
I hear, but cannot interpret!
It said something to me,
perhaps, of my dearest mother!
A quarrelsome dwarf
said to me once
he knew what the birds
were saying in song,
and men might find the meaning.
How could that really be?
Hey, I will try
after him;
on the reed echo his singing:
though lacking the meaning,
getting the mel'dy.
If I sing in his language,
perhaps I shall learn what he says.
(*He runs to the nearby spring, cuts off a reed
with his sword, and quickly makes a pipe of
it. He listens again.*)

He stops, and waits,
so now I will start!
(*He blows into the pipe, stops, and cuts the
pipe again. He blows again, shakes his head,
and again cuts the pipe. He tries it, gets
angry, presses the pipe with his hand, and
tries again. Then he stops and smiles.*)

The sound is false,
for my reed will not avail
for the beautiful tune.
Birdling, I think
my ear is dull;
'tis hard learning from you!
   (He hears the bird again, and looks up.)
The listening rascal
has made me feel shamefast!
He peers—and yet cannot get it!
Heida! just listen
now to my horn.
                    (He flings the pipe away.)
I am quite unskilled
with the stupid pipe.
I am better
at sounding a horn,
and here is a tune I can blow you;
I often have blown it,
calling for friends,
though none responded
but wolf and bear.
Now let me see
who comes when I call:
a trusty companion or friend.
*(He takes the silver hunting horn and blows,
then looks expectantly at the bird. There is a
movement in the background: Fafner, in the
form of a huge dragon has risen from his lair.
He breaks through the underbrush, and the
front part of his body becomes visible. He
utters a loud sound as if yawning. Siegfried
            looks at him in astonishment.)*
Ha ha! I see that my song
has attracted a beauty!
What a lovely comrade to have!

FAFNER.

Who is there?

SIEGFRIED.

Ei, are you a beast

that can speak to me?
Perhaps you can teach me something.
Here's a stripling
who knows no fear:
How would you like to teach me?

FAFNER.

Are you overbold?

SIEGFRIED.

Bold or overbold—
I know not!
But yet, teach me what fear is,
or you will forfeit your life.

FAFNER.
(with a sound like a laugh)

I was thristy,
Now too I find food!
(He opens his jaws and shows his teeth.)

SIEGFRIED.

Those are beautiful grinders,
pleasing to see;
wonderful teeth
for an ugly brute!
I really should close up the crater;
your jaws are open too wide.

FAFNER.

They're not much good
for empty talk;
yet I can eat you
with their aid.
(He lashes his tail menacingly.)

SIEGFRIED.

Hoho! you ugly,
horrible brute!
I have no mind
to fill your stomach.
Better, I think, to slay you
at once, without more delay.

FAFNER.
(roaring)

Pruh! Come,

insolent child!

SIEGFRIED.

Take care, roarer;
The boaster comes!
(*He draws his sword, springs toward Fafner
and waits defiant. Fafner drags himself
farther up on the knoll and spits from his
nostrils at Siegfried. Siegfried avoids the
slaver, springs nearer and stands to one side.
Fafner tries to flail him with his tail. Siegfried
leaps over him and wounds him in the tail.
Fafner roars, and rears up, so offering his
breast to the stroke. Siegfried sinks his sword
up to the hilt into his heart. Fafner sinks as
Siegfried lets go his sword and springs aside.*)
Lie there, merciless brute!
Needful lies in your vitals!

FAFNER.
(*weaker voice*)

Who are you, valiant stripling,
that have pierced my heart?
Who prompted your boyish will
to the murderous deed?
I know you did not plan
what you fulfilled.

SIEGFRIED.

Not much do I know,
not even who I am;
but you roused me to anger;
you were the cause of this strife.

FAFNER.

You bold, bright-eyed youngling,
unknown to yourself;
whom you have murdered,
hear from me.
The mighty giants of earth,
Fasolt and Fafner,
the brothers—both are now fallen;
for the cursed gold
bestowed by the gods,

made me murder my kin.
In dragon shape
I kept the treasure
Fafner, the last of the giants,
slain by a valorous boy!
Watch yourself well,
blossoming hero!
He who urged you blindly to this,
designs now your blossoming death!
Mark the ending!
Think of me!

(dying tone)

SIEGFRIED.

Who was my father,
answer me now;
show me your wisdom,
wild one, in dying.
Maybe my name can help you,
Siegfried, so am I called.

FAFNER.

Siegfried—

(He raises himself, and dies.)

SIEGFRIED.

The dead can tell no story.
So lead me henceforth,
my quickening sword!
(Fafner has rolled to one side in dying. Sieg-
fried draws the sword from his breast, and
in doing so his hand gets sprinkled with the
blood: he quickly pulls it back, and involun-
tarily carries his fingers to his mouth to suck
the blood from them. As he looks meditatively
before him his attention is suddenly attracted
by the bird's song.)
Like fire—burns my blood!
Really, it seems
as though I could hear the birds speak.
Is this effect
produced by the blood?
A strange and wondrous bird—

hark, what does he sing?

WOOD BIRD.
(from the branches of the lime tree above Siegfried)

> Hei! Siegfried now owns
> all the Nibelung's hoard;
> O, let him but find it
> within the cave!
> Let him but master the Tarnhelm,
> 'twill serve him for glorious deeds;
> but if he could master the ring,
> it would make him the lord of the world!

SIEGFRIED.
(softly, and with emotion)

> Thanks, dearest birdling,
> for your advice!
> I gladly will act!

(He turns, and descends into the cave, where he disappears.)

Mime slinks on, timidly looking about to assure himself that Fafner is dead. At the same moment Alberich appears from the cleft at the opposite side; he watches Mime narrowly. As the latter turns toward the cave he darts forward and bars his way.

ALBERICH.

Whereto slinking,
slippery wretch,
villainous knave?

MIME.

Accursed brother,
who wanted you!
What brings you here?

ALBERICH.

Greed is it, rogue,
and for my gold?
You covet my goods?

MIME.

Off with the nuisance!
The place here is mine:
so what do you want?

ALBERICH.

Have I then
interrupted the thief,
right in the act?

MIME.

What I achieved
through heavy toil,
shall not escape me.

ALBERICH.

Was it then you
who stole the gold from the Rhine?
And who gave the ring
its wondrous, magical might?

MIME.

Who made the Tarnhelm,
that changes the shapes of men?
I know you craved to,
but did you do it too?

ALBERICH.

What could you, you bungler,
ever have known how to fashion?
The magic ring
taught me that wonderful art.

MIME.

Where have you the ring?
You coward, the giants have seized it.
Now I will gain
by my cunning what you have lost.

ALBERICH.

Must you hoard with greed
what the stripling has won you?
But the boy is lord
of the radiant hoard, not you.

MIME.

I brought him up;
and he now pays for my pains
in toil and care.
My wait has been long for my wage.

ALBERICH.

For the youngling's care
will the beggarly,
scabby old knave
act so briskly brave,
think himself king?

I'd rather the ring
went to a
mangy dog than to you!
Lout that you are,
you'll never possess the ring!

MIME.
(scratches his head)

Well, keep it then,
and guard it well,
your shining ring;
be its lord,
but still call me your brother!
And for the Tarnhelm,
magical toy,
take it in trade;
then both are paid,
sharing the booty this way.

ALBERICH.
(with mocking laughter)

Share it with you?
And the Tarnhelm too?
How sly you are!
Then I'd never
sleep secure from your cunning!

MIME.
(beyond himself)

You'll not share it
Nor exchange it?
Nothing at all?
What do you mean—
Nothing for your poor brother?

ALBERICH.

Nothing, brother!
Mine is the treasure,
you shall not touch it.

MIME.
(furious)

Neither ring nor Tarnhelm
shall I allow you!
You shan't have a thing!

> I shall call for valiant Siegfried
> to help with his trusty sword;
> the dauntless boy
> will pay you, brother of mine!
> > *(Siegfried is visible in the background.)*

ALBERICH.

> Turn yourself round!
> He is coming now from the cave!

MIME.

> Surely by now
> he's taken the toys.
> *(Siegfried, with Tarnhelm and ring, has come
> slowly and meditatively from the cave. He
> regards his booty thoughtfully.)*

ALBERICH.

> He has the Tarnhelm.

MIME.

> Also the ring.

ALBERICH.

> Accurst! the ring?

MIME.
(laughing maliciously)

> Maybe he'll give you the circlet!
> and then I'll win it from you.
> *(With these words Mime slips away into the
> woods.)*

ALBERICH.

> The boy is its lord,
> Siegfried alone is its master.
> > *(He disappears into the cleft.)*

SIEGFRIED.

> What shall I do
> with the prize;
> I picked you out
> from the hoard of heaped up gold,
> because I heard that I should.
> At least you will serve
> as this day's reminder,
> to witness in truth
> that I finished Fafner in fight—

though still learning nothing of fear.
*(He puts the Tarnhelm in his girdle and the
ring on his finger. Silence. His attention is
again drawn to the bird, and he listens to it
with bated breath.)*

FOREST BIRD.

Hei! Siegfried is owner
of the helm and the ring!
O, let him not trust
in the villainous dwarf!
Let the stripling beware
of the rascal's treacherous tongue!
Now the boy can read
Mime's innermost mind.
the blood that he tasted is charmed.
*(Siegfried's gestures indicate that he has un-
derstood everything. He sees Mime coming
and remains without moving, leaning on his
sword, observing and self-contained.)*

MIME.
(creeps forward and observes Siegfried)

He broods and weighs
the booty's worth:
Maybe the Wanderer
used his wits
and came to this place
to wheedle the boy,
with cunning, crafty runes.
I must be
doubly on guard.
My cunning meshes
now must be laid,
so I with sugary,
truthless talk
may bamboozle the swaggering lad.
*(He advances nearer to Siegfried and wel-
comes him with flattering gestures.)*
Why! Welcome, Siegfried!
Say, my bold one,
what is the meaning of fear?

SIEGFRIED.

No teacher yet have I found.

MIME.

But the dragon foe,
tell, have you destroyed him?
He was quite a playmate, no doubt?

SIEGFRIED.

Though quite a terrible foe,
his death grieves me at heart
when far wickeder rogues
remain alive and unpunished.
The one who led me here
I hate still more than the foe!

MIME.
(very friendly)

Now gently! I come
to bid you goodbye:
for soon shall death
close your eyes in endless sleep.
You've done what I wanted,
finished your chore;
now all that I need
is merely to win the booty.
I think that task will be simple,
you are really easy to fool.

SIEGFRIED.

You think then to do me mischief?

MIME.
(astonished, tenderly)

Now did I say that?
Siegfried, hear me, my baby!
Hate is in my heart:
you were always my loathing!
You nuisance, I wasted
no love upon you;
I toiled for the gold alone,
the treasure hid in Fafner's cave.
(as though he were promising him pleasant
                                          things)

Either give it

right now to my care,
Siegfried, my son,
or see for yourself,

(with friendly humor)

you'll lose your life in a hurry!

SIEGFRIED.

That you do hate me,
gives me joy:
yet must my life as well then be forfeit?

MIME.
(crossly)

Now did I say that?
You don't hear me aright!

(He feels for his bottle.)

See, you are weary,
from heavy toil.
Fever burns hot in your blood;
so, to refresh you,
with quickening drink
Mime wasted no time;
while you welded your sword,
I brewed you this broth;
now, if you drink,
your sword then will fall to me,
and with it helm and hoard!
Hi hi hi hi hi!

SIEGFRIED.

You plot for my sword
and all I have fought for—
ring, and helmet, and booty?

MIME.
(violently)

Why is your hearing so bad!
Tell me, do I but dote?
I subtly take
the greatest of pains
to keep my thoughts secret,
cunningly hidden,
and you, stupid booby,
twist my words all awry!

Open your ears, child,
and attend to me!
Listen to Mime's words!
   (again very friendly, with evident pains)
Here, take, and drink for refreshment!
My drinks always were good:
when you were fretful,
peevish and cross,
they quenched your thirst.
You always took what I offered.

SIEGFRIED.
(without stirring)

Now a tasty drink
would be fine.
But how has this one been brewed?

MIME.
(jesting merrily, as if describing a pleasant intoxication)

Hey, just drink it,
trust to my skill,
and soon your thoughts
will sink into darkness and night!
It will stretch your body stiff,
making it senseless.
There as you lie,
no trouble for me
to pilfer the booty:
but if you should awake,
I would nowhere
find myself safe,
though the ring were my own.
Then, with the sword
that you made so sharp,
         (with a gesture of exuberant joy)
off will I hack
your head, my child.
Then peace will be mine, also the ring!
Hi-hi-hi-hi-hi-hi-hi-hi-hi-hi-hi!

SIEGFRIED.

So while I sleep you would slay me?

MIME.
(very angrily)

Now really! Did I say that?
(He takes pains to express the tenderest
tones.)

I wish, my child,
but to have your head!
(in tone of heartfelt solicitude for Siegfried's
health)

For, even without
my rooted hate,
which grew from your scorn
at my shameful labor,
and cries aloud for vengeance,
I would clear you from my pathway!
Faltering would not suit me!

(again jestingly)

How else could I come by the booty,
which Alberich covets as well?
(He pours the draught into the drinking horn
and offers it to Siegfried with importunate
gestures.)

Now, my Volsung!
Wolf son, eh?
Drink, and choke to your death!
This drink will be your last!
Hi-hi-hi-hi-hi!
(Siegfried threatens him with the sword.)

SIEGFRIED.

Taste of my sword,
sickening babbler!
(As if seized by violent loathing he thrusts
his sword into Mime. The dwarf falls dead.)

ALBERICH'S VOICE.
(heard from the cleft in mocking laughter)

Ha-ha-ha-ha-ha-ha-ha-ha-ha-ha-ha-ha-ha!

SIEGFRIED.
(As he looks at Mime on the ground he returns his sword to its
belt.)

Needful pays
hate's wages:

that is why it was fashioned.

*(He picks up Mime's body and carries it to
the knoll in front of the cave, then throws it
into the cave.)*

In the cavern here
lie on the hoard!
You sought the gold
with resolute craft;
now may you have joy of your treasure!
You may keep this trusty
guardian too,
thus you're protected from thieves.

*(With mighty efforts he pushes the body of
the dragon in front of the entrance to the
cave so as to stop it up completely.)*

Now lie there too,
dragon foe!
Take care of the hoard,
share in its watch
with your booty-coveting mate:
and so I leave you both in peace.

*(He looks thoughtfully into the cave, and then
turns, as though tired. He passes his hand
over his brow.)*

Hot am I
from the heavy toil.
Rushing flows
my fev'rish blood!
My hand burns on my head.
High is the sun already;
the shining eye
lights up heaven
and beats right down on my head.
By the lime tree
I'll find refreshment and shelter.

*(He stretches out again under the lime tree.
Great silence. Then woodland murmurs.)*

Still once more, dearest birdling,
whom we have
disturbed with our noise,

I would love to hear your singing.
You are rocking with the branches
so gaily; chirping and chattering.
Brothers and sisters,
fly round you in gladness and love!
Yet I—am so alone,
lacking brother and sister.
My dear mother died,
my father fell—
unknown by their son.
My one only friend
was a villainous dwarf;
love did never grow from nearness;
treacherous tricks
were planned by this plotter,
and so I was forced to slay him.

(He again looks up at the branches.)

Generous birdling,
just tell me this now:
could you find
a loving friend for me?
Can you give me helpful counsel?
I often have called,
and yet no one has come.
You, my faithful,
surely could find one:
you always counsel me well.

(softly)

Now sing! I'll listen to your song.

WOOD BIRD.

Hei! Siegfried has struck down
the wicked dwarf!
Now, soon he may take
a wonderful wife.
She sleeps surrounded by fire,
high on a mountain of rock:
who steps through the flames
wakens the bride,
Brunnhilda then may be his.

(Siegfried starts up impetuously.)

SIEGFRIED.

O gracious song!
Sweetest of strains!
I feel its thought
burn in my breast!
It stirs me strongly,
kindling my heart!
What courses so fast
through heart and senses?
Sing it to me, gentle friend!

WOOD BIRD.

Happy but sad
I sing of love.
joyful from woe,
weaving my song:
through longing alone can one hear.

SIEGFRIED.

Joy takes me,
now that I wander
forth from the wood to the rock!
Yet once more answer me,
gracious singer:
Shall I then break through the fire?
Can I awaken the bride?

(He listens again.)

WOOD BIRD.

Who wins the bride,
Brunnhild the fair,
no coward he:
there is one lacking in fear!

SIEGFRIED.

The stupid boy
who has never known fear,
my birdling, why that is I!
I toiled this day
to learn fear, but in vain.
My foe was unable to teach me:
I'm burning with joy
now to learn it from Brunnhilda.
What way shall I take to the rock?

(The bird flutters up, circles over Siegfried,
and flies hesitatingly before him.)

So I see the path is shown me:
My ready footsteps
follow your flight!

(He runs after the bird, who for a time teases him by leading
him in different directions; then it takes a definite direction and
Siegfried follows.)

Night, a wild spot at the foot of a steeply rising rocky mountain. Storm, lightning and violent thunder, which soon ceases, while the lightning continues to flash among the clouds. Here the Wanderer enters. He walks deliberately toward the mouth of a cavernous opening in a rock in the foreground, and stands there, leaning on his sword.

WANDERER.

Waken, Vala!
Vala, awake!
Awake from sleep;
wake from the cavern of night!
Arise as I call!
Arise! arise!
From vaults of the earth,
from shadowy caverns arise!
Erda! Erda!
Ancient of days!
From tenebrous darkness
soar to the light!
I sing to wake you
from dreams of wisdom;
so wake from your visions;
wake at my call!
All-knowing one!

Wisdom's mother!
Erda! Erda!
Ancient of days!
Waken, awaken, you Vala! Awaken!
(*The cavern begins to glow with a bluish
light. Very gradually Erda rises from below,
appearing as if covered with hoar-frost, while
her hair and garments shimmer.*)

ERDA.

Strong is the song!
Mighty magic stirs me!
I am aroused
from knowledge in dreams.
Who dares to rob my rest?

WANDERER.

Your wakener is here;
my songs have power
to waken surely
the dreamer locked in sleep.
I roam the planet,
wandering much,
questing for knowledge
prime wisdom comes if we seek it.
There is no being
wiser than you;
you know what lies
in the depths of earth,
what hill and dale,
air and water surround.
Where life is found,
there lives your spirit.
Where minds are thinking,
your mind thinks too.
Boundless knowledge
lives in your soul.
So I have come here for counsel,
driving sleep from your eyes!

ERDA.

My sleep is dreaming,
my dreaming thinking,

my thinking power of knowing.
Yet while I sleep
the Norns are wakeful:
they weave the rope,
and truly spin what I know;
so why not ask the sisters?

WANDERER.

They weave as they must:
nothing can turn them.
The world by fate holds them in
        thralldom.
And so I ask you,
mother of wisdom,
how to hinder a rolling wheel.

ERDA.

Deeds of men
cast a shadow on my soul;
my wisdom itself
once felt a conqueror's force.
A wish-maiden
I bore to Wotan:
she brought to Valhall
the heroes he asked for.
Bold is she
and wise as well.
Why waken me
and ask no counsel from
Erda's and Wotan's child?

WANDERER.

You mean then the Valkyr,
Brunnhilda, the maid?
She flouted the master of tempests,
when he was showing most self-control:
what the guider of strife
desired with longing,
yet what he refrained from
in spite of himself,
that did the maid,
proud in her confidence,

try herself to accomplish,
right in the thick of the fray.
War-father
punished the maid;
cast a sleeping spell on her eyes;
she is resting on the rock.
The only one to waken the child
will be the man who wins her as bride.
What could I learn from the maid?

ERDA.

My waking
makes me confused.
Wild and strange
seems the world!
The Valkyrie,
the Vala child,
paid, by fetters of sleep,
while her all-knowing mother slept!
Why should pride's teacher
punish pride?
Why should he who urged her
scowl at the deed,
he who guards the right,
and upholds all pledges,
strike at the right,
rule by falsehood?
Let my wisdom seek slumber!

WANDERER.

You, Mother, shall not go free,
for a mighty magic is mine.
All-knowing,
since you did thrust
a thorn of sorrow
in Wotan's resolute heart,
you filled his spirit,
telling of shameful,
direful destruction,
and bound his being with fear.
Are you the world's

wisest of women?
Answer me then
how the god may master his woe!

ERDA.

You are—not
what you have said!
Wild spirit, why have you come here
to trouble the Vala's sleep?

WANDERER.

You are not
what you believe.
Prime-wisdom marches
to its downfall;
your knowledge depends
upon my wishes.
Tell me what Wotan wills.

(Long silence.)

Unwise one,
I cry in your ear,
forever may you sleep in peace!
The eternals' downfall
gives me no anguish,
since I willed it so.
What I resolved in painful sorrow,
with wild despair in my heart,
glad and joyful
now I freely bring on.
Though in my scorn I devoted
the world to the Nibelungs' greed,
the noblest of Volsungs
now may inherit from me.
One who never knew me,
yet chosen by me,
a valorous stripling,
without my teaching,
has won the Nibelungs' ring.
Free from hate,
happy in loving,
the boy is not harmed

by Alberich's curse.
He knows nothing of fear.
She you bore to me,
Brunnhilda,
will be waked by him:
then your wisdom's child
shall perform a deed
to redeem the world.
So finish your sleep,
shut fast your eyelids:
dream and behold my downfall.
Whatever these young ones
may bring to pass,
to that I joyfully yield.
So down then, Erda!
Prime mother fear!
First sorrow!
Go down, go down
to endless sleep!

(Erda who, with closed eyes, has already begun to sink, now entirely disappears. The cavern is again quite dark. Dawn illumines the stage; the storm is over.)

SECOND SCENE

The Wanderer has come to the cave and is leaning with his back against the rocks.

WANDERER.

I see that Siegfried comes.
(Siegfried's wood bird flutters in, suddenly stops, flutters about in alarm and then disappears quickly. Siegfried enters and stops.)

SIEGFRIED.

My birdling flew from my sight!
With fluttering flight
and sweetest song
blithely he showed me the way,
and now he's flown far away!
So I must
find out the rock by myself.
My birdling showed me the way,
that way shall be my path.
(He starts to go.)

WANDERER.

Whereto, fellow?
What do you seek?

SIEGFRIED.
(stopping and turning)

Did someone speak?
Perhaps he knows the way.
There's a mountain guarded

237

by raging fire, and I seek it.
There sleeps a maid
whom I must awake.

WANDERER.

Who told you though
to seek the mountain?
Who caused you to long for the woman?

SIEGFRIED.

I heard a singing
wood birdling
who gave me welcome counsel.

WANDERER.

A wood bird chatters idly;
no man can hear the words.
So how could you tell
what tale he sang you?

SIEGFRIED.

The magic was worked
by a dragon's blood,
destroyed at hate-cave before me.
His burning blood
scarce had wet my tongue,
when I fathomed the song of the bird.

WANDERER.

Who urged you on to fight
the giant foe,
the mighty dragon you slew?

SIEGFRIED.

Old Mime urged me,
a wily dwarf,
who tried to teach me what fear is;
but what did urge me
most was the beast;
he was the cause himself,
with his ugly, threatening jaws.

WANDERER.

Who made the sword
so sharp and hard
that it slew the fiercest foe?

SIEGFRIED.

I forged it myself,
for the goblin could not:
else would I still lack a sword.

WANDERER.

Yet who made
the mighty pieces
with which you made the needed sword?

SIEGFRIED.

I really can't tell.
I only know
that unless the pieces were put together
the sword would not serve.

WANDERER.
(with a good-humored laugh)

That surely is true!
(He looks at Siegfried with pleasure.)

SIEGFRIED.
(surprised)

Now why do you laugh?
Busybody,
hear once for all,
keep me no longer here prating.
If you can help
direct me, then do so;
if not, old man,
then close your jaw!

WANDERER.

Keep calm, young fellow!
If I seem old,
then show me honor, respect me.

SIEGFRIED.

That is a good one!
My whole life long
there stood in my path
an ancient fellow;
now I have swept him away.
If you stand longer
barring me my pathway,
then take care, old one,

lest that you perish, like him.
> (*He steps nearer the Wanderer.*)

How odd you appear!
Why do you wear
such a monstrous hat?
Also, why does it cover your face?

WANDERER.
(*without changing his position*)
> Thus does the Wanderer wear it
> when he goes against the wind.

SIEGFRIED.
(*examining him still more closely*)
> But an eye beneath it is lacking!
> So doubtless some one
> Once put it out
> when you were stubborn
> and barred his way.
> Make yourself scarce,
> or else you may quickly
> lose your other eye also.

WANDERER.

> Although you know
> nothing, my son,
> you know at least your cock-sureness!
> With the one eye
> that is missing in me,
> you look yourself on the other
> that still is left me for sight.

SIEGFRIED.

> Ha ha ha ha!
> You make me laugh with your nonsense!
> Yet hear, I trifle no longer;
> be quick, show me the way,
> then pursue your own way yourself!
> For that's all
> you're good for, I think.
> So speak, or out of my path!

WANDERER.
(gently)

> Child, if you knew
> who I am
> your scoff—would have been spared!
> Painful it is
> when a dear one so threatens!
> Long have I loved
> your radiant race,
> though it felt fear
> at my furious wrath.
> You, whom I love so—
> all too noble—
> do not waken my wrath;
> it would ruin both you and me!

SIEGFRIED.

> Still you won't tell,
> stubborn old man?
> Out of my way, then;
> for that way, I know,
> leads to the maid on the rock.
> The wood bird has shown me,
> who right here took off in flight.

WANDERER.
(breaking out in anger)

> It fled you to save its life!
> It thought the ruler
> of ravens near.
> Too bad, should he get caught!
> The way he directed,
> shall you not take!

SIEGFRIED.
(surprised, steps back defiantly)

> Hoho! you forbidder!
> Who are you then
> that you would bar my way?

WANDERER.

> Guard yourself from the guardian!
> The sleeping maid
> of the rock is chained by my might.

He who would wake her,
he who would win her,
mightless makes me forever!
A flaming sea
encircles the maid.
Flickering fires
lick round the rock.
He who craves the bride
must walk through flames to the rock.
(He points with his spear.)
Look toward the heights
and gaze at that light!
Its splendor grows,
its glowing swells,
clouds there are scorching,
fires there are flick'ring,
rolling and burning,
and raging this way.
A light sea
illumines your head;
enkindling flames
can seize and devour you.
Go back then, foolhardy boy!

SIEGFRIED.

Go back, you babbler, yourself!
There, where the blaze is burning,
is Brunnhilda, whom I must find.
*(He moves onward. The Wanderer bars his
way.)*

WANDERER.

Have you no fear of the fire?
Why then I must hinder your way!
For still do I hold
the mighty haft.
The sword that you swing
once broke upon this shaft;
yet once again
let it splinter upon this spear!
(He stretches out his spear.)

SIEGFRIED.
(drawing his sword)

> So my father's foe
> faces me here?
> Sweet is the vengeance
> that comes my way!
> Swing with your spear,
> and let it split on my sword!
> *(With one stroke he hews the spear in two pieces, from which a flash of lightning shoots up toward the rocky heights, where the ever brightening flames begin to be visible. A loud thunderclap accompanies the stroke. The Wanderer quietly picks up the pieces, which have fallen at his feet.)*

WANDERER.

> Fare on! I cannot prevent you!
> *(He disappears into the darkness.)*

SIEGFRIED.

> When his spear is done for,
> see how he flees me!
> *(The growing brightness of the clouds meets his sight.)*
>
> Ha! gladdening glow!
> glorious light,
> lighting my pathway
> clearly before me!
> I'll bathe in the fire!
> I'll go through the flames to my bride!
> Ho-ho! Ha-hei!
> Again let me call you mate!

(He puts his horn to his lips and plunges into the waving fire which flows down from the heights. He is soon out of sight, and is apparently ascending the mountain.)

THIRD SCENE

The glow sinks to a fine transparent veil, which also clears off, revealing a lovely blue sky and bright weather. The scene, from which all the vapors have fled, represents the summit of a rocky mountain peak: left, the entrance to a natural rocky hall; right, spreading fir trees; foreground, beneath the shade of a spreading fir tree, lies Brunnhilda in deep sleep. She is in complete armor.

Siegfried has now reached the rocky heights in the background. He looks around, astonished.

SIEGFRIED.

Blessed this haven
on sun-brightened height!
(He mounts to the top of the height. Then he looks into the wood, and comes a little forward.)

What rests there sleeping
mid shades of the firs?
A charger,
lying in heavy sleep.
(Coming nearer he stops in surprise.)
What flashes there upon me?
What glistening steel is that?
Maybe the flames
still dazzle my sight.
Shining armor?
Here, let me see.
(He lifts up the shield and sees Brunnhilda's form.)

245

Ha! in armor—a man?
The sight is pleasant to see!
His helmet's tight,
pressing his head.
He would rest
the easier thus.
*(He carefully loosens the helmet and lifts it
from the head of the sleeper; long curling
hair breaks forth. Siegfried starts.)*
Ah! how fair!
Shimmering clouds
encircle in fleeces
a radiant, heavenly sea;
laughing, the dazzling
face of the sun
streams through the billowy clouds.
(He bends lower over the sleeper.)
The labor to breathe
is heaving his breast,
so let me loosen his corslet.

(He tries.)

Come, my sword!
Cut through the iron.
*(Drawing his sword, he gently cuts through
the rings, then lifts off the breastplate, so that
Brunnhilda lies before him in a soft woman's
dress. Startled and astonished, he draws
back.)*

That is no man!
Burning bewitchment
pierces my heart!
Fiery pangs
rivet my eyesight!
My thoughts are reeling from fear!
Now whom shall I call,
that he may help me?
Mother! Mother!
Remember me!
*(He sinks as if fainting on Brunnhilda's
bosom. Then he starts up, sighing.)*

How waken the maid,
to see her eyes when they open—
those eyes, when they open?

(tenderly)

Might not her look make me blind?
How could I dare
endure such a light?
All swims, and rocks,
and staggers, and whirls!
Anguish of longing
weakens my spirit!
My hand on my heart
is trembling with fear!
What ails me, coward!
Is this what fear means?
O Mother! Mother!
Your dauntless child!

(very gently)

A woman, resting asleep
has taught him the meaning of fear!
And now I'd unknow
the fear I know!
So, if I'm to waken,
then the maid must be wakened.
*(He is overcome with tender emotions. He
bends down deeper.)*

Sweetly quivers
her blossoming mouth!
Its gentle trembling
has banished my fear.
Ah! and the warm
and blissful scent of her breath!

(as if in despair)

Awaken! Awaken!
Holiest maid!

(He gazes at her.)

She hears me not.
But life I will gather
as bees gather honey;
what though I die for the deed!

(He sinks, as if dying, on the sleeping figure, and fastens his lips on hers. Brunnhilda opens her eyes. Siegfried rises and remains standing before her. Slowly she rises to a sitting position. As her consciousness returns she greets heaven and earth with stately gestures.)

BRUNNHILDA.

Hail, O sun-lord!
Hail, O light!
Hail, O radiant day!
Long was my sleep;
I am awake.
Who is the hero
that broke my sleep?

SIEGFRIED.

It was I who reached the rock
through walls of fire.
It was I who undid your helm,
Siegfried it was
who broke your sleep.

BRUNNHILDA.

Gods, I hail you!
Hail, O world!
Hail, O earth in your glory!
My sleep is at an end;
my life wakens.
Siegfried is it
through whom I wake.

SIEGFRIED.

O hail to her
who gave me my birth!

BRUNNHILDA.

O hail to her
who gave you your birth!

SIEGFRIED.

Hail to earth
that fostered my life!

BRUNNHILDA.

Hail to earth
that fostered your life.

SIEGFRIED.

letting me see those eyes
that kindly bless as they laugh!

BRUNNHILDA.

Your gaze alone dared behold me,
for none could wake me but you!
*(Both remain filled with glowing ecstasy, lost
in mutual contemplation.)*
O Siegfried, Siegfried!
Glorious youth!
O waker of life,
victorious light!
O, did you know, joy of the world,
how I have always loved you!
You were my gladness,
my watchful care!
Your life was sheltered
before it was yours.
My shield was your buckler
before you were born.
So long was my love, Siegfried.

SIEGFRIED.

My mother did not die then?
Was she only asleep?

BRUNNHILDA.
(smiles, stretching forth her hand to him in a friendly manner)
You wonderful child,
no more your mother will greet you.
We are as one,
if I am blessed by your love.
What you would know
lies in my soul;
yet only with my love
rises my wisdom!
O Siegfried! Siegfried!
I loved you always,
for I alone
divined my father's intention:
though I never dared to think
or to name it,

I guarded silence,
feeling it only;
and for it fought,
battled and strove;
and for it flouted
him who conceived it;
and so I suffered
penance in sleep;
yet I did not think it,
but only felt!
For, what the thought was—
might you discern it—
was only my love for you!

SIEGFRIED.

How joyful sounds
your wonderful song!
And yet the meaning seems dark.
I can see your shining
lustrous eyes;
I can feel your warm and gentle breath,
and the song you sing
is sweet to hear:
yet what you say as you sing,
wondering I cannot grasp.
I cannot grasp clearly
thoughts in the distance,
when all my senses
feel and see you only!
A heavy fear
fetters my heart:
a fear that you only
taught me to know;
so you, who bound me
in mightiest fetters,
give me my courage again!

BRUNNHILDA.
(looking toward the wood)

I see my Grane,
my sacred steed:

he slept by my side,
now he grazes there.
He too was awakened by you.

SIEGFRIED.

My eyes love to graze
on lips that are lovely:
my own are athirst
to taste of their sweetness,
and to know the joys of that pasture!

BRUNNHILDA.
(indicating her weapons)

I see there the shield
that guarded heroes.
I see there the helmet
that hid my head:
it shields, it guards me no more.

SIEGFRIED.

A heavenly maid
has wounded my heart;
wounds from a woman
throb in my head.
I came without shield or helm!

BRUNNHILDA.
(sadly)

I see there the corslet's
shimmering steel:
a keen-edged sword
cut it in two;
with its glittering edge
you loosened the mail.
No corslet or shield is left
to the weak, the sorrowful maid!

SIEGFRIED..

I battled through fire,
to get to your side;
no corslet or armor
guarded my life:
and now the flames
have pierced to my breast.
My blood runs hot

in turbulent streams;
a ravening fire
is kindled within me.
The flame that shone
round Brunnhild's rock
is burning now in my breast!
O maid! extinguish the fire!
Quiet its simmering rage!

(*He embraces her impetuously.*)

BRUNNHILDA.
(*resisting him with the utmost strength of terror, and flying to
the other side of the stage*)

No god neared me then!
The heroes showed
obeisance to Brunnhild:
holy came she from Valhall.
Woe's me! Woe's me!
Woe for the shame,
the bitter disgrace!
For he who woke me
gives me the wound!
He has broken corslet and helm:
Brunnhilda am I no more!

SIEGFRIED.

You still are
but the slumbering maid:
Brunnhilda lies
still in her sleep.
Awaken! Be now a wife!

BRUNNHILDA.

My senses are reeling,
my reason fails:
shall all my wisdom vanish?

SIEGFRIED.

Did you not sing
that wisdom was
your glorious love for myself?

BRUNNHILDA.

Deepening darkness
troubles my sight;

My eyes are dimming.
My light dies out,
night fills my heart.
Through horror and gloom,
writhing and raging,
comes frenzied fear;
terror screeches
and rears itself high!
(She impetuously hides her eyes with her hands.)

SIEGFRIED.
(gently taking her hands away from her eyes)

Night enfolds
imprisoned eyes.
When the fetters vanish,
the fears do too.
Dive through the darkness and see:
bright with the sun blazes the day!

BRUNNHILDA.

Bright with the sun
blazes the day of my shame!
O Siegfried! Siegfried!
See how I fear!
(Her manner shows that a pleasing picture has come to her mind. She looks tenderly on Siegfried.)

Life was given me,
life eternal,
endless in sweet
rapturous longing—
yet only to make you blest.
O Siegfried! Glorious!
Hoard of the world!
Hero most holy!
Light of the world!
Leave, ah, leave,
leave me alone!
Come not to me
in your passionate longing.
Conquer me not

with your mastering might!
O, bring me not ruin and shame!
Have you not felt
an eager joy
to see your face in the brook?
Yet if you trouble
the slumbering waves,
and shatter the quiet smile
of the brook,
your face then must be lost—
nothing left but turmoil of waves.
So inflict not your will,
trouble me not!
Like the brook
let me mirror back
your picture in beauty,
brave and joyous young man!
O Siegfried! radiant child!
Love yourself,
and leave me alone;
destroy not the one you own!

SIEGFRIED.

I love you.
O, might you love me!
No more am I mine:
O, would you were mine!
Before me
a wondrous river rolls:
with all my senses
I only see
its joyous, billowing waters.
If it will not
reflect back my face,
still would I plunge
in the cooling water,
myself, as I am,
ending my pains:
O that its billows
might drown me in bliss,

and quench my fire with its waves!
Awaken, Brunnhilda!
Waken, O maid!
laughing and living,
sweetest delight!
Be mine! be mine! be mine!

BRUNNHILDA.

O Siegfried! yours
ever I've been!

SIEGFRIED.

Mine have you been,
then be mine now!

BRUNNHILDA.

Yours always
will I be!

SIEGFRIED.

What you will be,
be to me now!
Tight in my arms
I hold you embraced,
thus with my breast
feeling your heartbeats;
glances are kindling,
gently we mingle breath,
eyes to eyes
and mouth to mouth!
Then are you to me
what always you were and will be!
The fear and the passion would vanish,
if now Brunnhild were mine.

BRUNNHILDA.

If I were yours?
Godlike repose
is tossing in tumult;
chastity's light
blazes to passion:
heavenly wisdom
flees far away;
jubilant love

is driving it hence!
If I am yours?
Siegfried! Siegfried!
Do you not see?
Does the fire of my eye
not blind you with light?
When I hold you close
are you not burned?
When my turbulent blood
is surging toward you,
the raging fire,
can you not feel?
Do you not, Siegfried—
do you not fear
the wild, amorous maid?

SIEGFRIED.

Ha!
As my glowing blood is enkindled,
as our burning glances are meeting,
as I clasp you, blazing with ardor,
surely my courage
comes again;
and the fear, ah!
I had failed to learn,
the fear you had
hardly skill to teach,
that terror—that fear,
has vanished and left me a fool!

BRUNNHILDA.

O valorous child,
O wonderful hero!
you simple lord
of glorious deeds!
Laughing must I love you,
laughing let me be blinded,
laughing let us be lost,
and laughing descend to doom!

SIEGFRIED.

Laughing awake

in gladness to me!

BRUNNHILDA.

Farewell, Valhall's
radiant world!
Let fall your glittering
towers to dust!

SIEGFRIED.

Brunnhilda lives,
Brunnhilda laughs!
Hail, O day
that shines all around us!

BRUNNHILDA.

Farewell, glistening
pomp of the gods!

SIEGFRIED.

Hail, O sun
that gives us the day!

BRUNNHILDA.

End in rapture,
you eternal race!

SIEGFRIED.

Hail, O light,
that have burst from night!

BRUNNHILDA.

Now rend, you Norns,
your rope of runes!

SIEGFRIED.

Hail, O world,
where Brunnhilda lives!

BRUNNHILDA.

Dusk of gods,
enfold us around!

SIEGFRIED.

She wakes! she lives!

BRUNNHILDA.

Night of their downfall,
come with the mist!

SIEGFRIED.

She greets me with laughter.
Proudly shines

my Brunnhilda's star!

BRUNNHILDA.

I see, still shining,
Siegfried's star!

SIEGFRIED.

She is mine always
and forever mine,
and mine alone—my all!

BRUNNHILDA.

He is mine always
and forever mine,
and mine alone—my all!
Love that enlightens!
Death that is joy!
Love that enlightens!
Death that is joy!
(She throws herself in Siegfried's arms.)

SIEGFRIED.

Love that enlightens!
Death that is joy!
Love that enlightens!
Death that is joy!

THE END

THE TWILIGHT OF THE GODS

CHARACTERS

THE THREE NORNS *(the Fates)*

SIEGFRIED

BRUNNHILDA

GUNTHER, *King of the Gibichungs*

GUTRUNA, *His Sister*

HAGEN, *Son of Alberich*

VALTRAUTA, *Valkyrie Sister of Brunnhilda*

ALBERICH

THE THREE RHINE-DAUGHTERS

VASSALS AND WOMEN

THE TWILIGHT OF THE GODS

PRELUDE

The Valkyrie's Rock

The same scene as at the end of Siegfried. *It is night, and from below, at back, gleams the fire.*

The three Norns, tall women in somber and flowing drapery, are discovered. The first is crouching under the spreading fir tree; the second is stretched out on a rock before the cave; the third sits on a rock below the peak.

FIRST NORN.

What light glimmers there?

SECOND NORN.

Is it the dawn so soon?

THIRD NORN.

Loge's host
dances flaming round the rock.
Night's still here.
Let's on with our spinning and song.

SECOND NORN.
(to the first)

While we are spinning and singing
the cord has to be stretched.

FIRST NORN.
(rises and fastens one end of a golden cord to a branch of the fir tree while she sings)

Though all goes well and ill,

fasten the cord while singing.
At the world ash tree
once I wove,
when, lush and thick,
the stem put forth
with holy and verdurous boughs.
Amid cool shadows
purled a spring.
Whispering wisdom
rippled its waves.
I sang my mystical thoughts.
A valiant god
stepped to drink at the spring,
and he yielded up an eye
as his payment for power.
From the world ash tree
Wotan broke away a branch.
From this wood the hero
shaped the shaft of a spear.
The course of time was long.
Worse grew the wound in the wood.
Leaves fell in their sereness.
Then, blight took the tree.
Sadly the source of the water failed.
All my songs
were measures of woe.
And now no more do I weave beside the
        ash.
So must the fir tree
serve me for fastening the cord.
Sing, O sister—
you take it now—
why was all this so?

SECOND NORN.
(winding the cord thrown to her round a projecting rock at the cave's mouth)

Wotan carved on his
mighty spear-shaft
runes stating

truth to pacts must hold.
This haft of the world was his.
A valiant man
destroyed his spear in the strife.
The binding witness
to pacts was shattered to bits.
With that, Wotan
bade his heroes
to hew down the ash
with its boughs,
and to shiver all to splinters.
The ash tree fell.
Evermore dried was the spring.
Therefore the jut
of this rock must hold my cord.
Sing, O sister—
you catch it now—
why is all this so?

THIRD NORN.
(catching the cord and casting the end behind her)
The giants' work
yet towers aloft.
There sits Wotan,
and with him
all his assembly,
holy heroes and gods.
A heap of billets piled up high
forms a pyre
round all the castle.
The world ash tree waits the torch!
When the wood
blazes up to the sky,
when the flame
eats up the glittering hall,
the gods everlasting
will have reached the dusk of their day.
Would you know more?
Then wind up the cord once again.
And catch it now,

it comes from the north.
Spin, O sister, while singing.
(She throws the cord to the second Norn,
who throws it to the first.)

FIRST NORN.
(unties the cord from the branch and fastens it to another
branch while she sings.)

Is that the dawn
or a flickering glimmer?
My woe darkens my gaze.
I scarce remember
the ancient marvels.
When Loge once
broke out into brilliant flame,
tell me, what was his fate?

SECOND NORN.
(again taking the cord, and winding it round the stone)

Through the spear's strong magic
Wotan has tamed him.
Loge whispered his lore.
But to gain his freedom,
seizing the spear
he gnawed the runes with his teeth.
Then with the spear-point's
mastering magic,
Wotan made Loge
blaze round the rock of Brunnhilda.
Do you know why this is?

THIRD NORN.
(catching the cord again and casting it behind her)

Soon will Wotan,
taking splints of his spear-shaft,
drive them deep
in the breast of the fiery god.
Then with the brand
flaming away,
the god will kindle
the world ash tree
heaped high in billets and faggots.
When will this, though,

come to pass?
Stretch now, sisters, the cord!
(She throws the cord to the second, who in turn throws it to the first.)

FIRST NORN.
(again knotting the cord)

The night wanes.
Nothing comes further.
I cannot find
the strands of the cord.
The braided work is undone.
A terrible sight
puts my thoughts in a whirl:
the dwarf has robbed
the gold of the Rhine.
Tell me, what was his fate?

SECOND NORN.
(winding the rope round the stone)

The stone is sharply
cutting the cord.
The spun thread holds
no more as it did:
the web now is awry.
The Nibelung ring
fills me with pain and distress.
A furious curse
gnaws on the strands of my cord.
Tell me what things will come.

THIRD NORN.
(hastily catching the cord thrown to her)

The cord is too slack!
It does not stretch!
If I'm to send it northward
it must be stretched
much tighter than that.
(She pulls on the cord, and it breaks.)

SECOND NORN.

It breaks!

THIRD NORN.

It breaks!

FIRST NORN.

It breaks!

ALL THREE.

Thus ends wisdom eternal!
The world marks
our wisdom no more.
Away, to Mother, away!

(They disappear.)

*(The day, which has been gradually breaking,
now dawns brightly, thus concealing the distant fire-glow in the valley.)*

*(Siegfried and Brunnhilda enter from the
cave. Siegfried is in full armor; Brunnhilda is
leading her horse by the bridle.)*

BRUNNHILDA.

Unless I left you,
dearest, O hero,
to new exploits,
poor were my love.
A single doubt, though,
still constrains me:
the fear that all
I have given is slight.
I gave you my wisdom
from the gods,
lore from my hoard
of holy runes;
yet you have robbed
the staff of my strength,
my maidenly might.
Now it is gone,
and I live to serve you.
My wisdom's gone,
but my will remains.
I'm rich in love
but lacking in strength.
Do not despise
the wretched woman

who only wishes,
but cannot perform.

SIEGFRIED.

More have you given me
than I have wit to know.
So chide not, if your lessons
have left me still untaught.
One thing though I know quite well:
for me Brunnhilda lives.
One thing's not too hard to learn:
Brunnhilda to remember!

BRUNNHILDA.

If you would prove you love me,
recall the goal you had.
Recall your deeds of valor.
Recall the magic fire
you stepped through in your daring,
when it blazed around the rock!

SIEGFRIED.

Brunnhilda was my purpose!

BRUNNHILDA.

Recall, too, the maid with the shield,
whom you found in magic slumber,
and whose fastened helmet you broke.

SIEGFRIED.

Brunnhilda thus was wakened!

BRUNNHILDA.

Recall the pledges
that unite us.
Recall the troths
that we have plighted.
Recall the love
that we have lived by.
Then Brunnhild's holy flame
will ever burn in your breast!
(She embraces Siegfried.)

SIEGFRIED.

Now I leave you, my love,
in the blest protection of fire.
For secret runes you taught me

take this ring in exchange.
All the deeds I ever did
obtained their virtue here.
I once conquered a dragon foe
who grimly guarded this ring.
Now keep this powerful charm
as holy pledge of my troth!

BRUNNHILDA.

I'll cherish it more than all else.
For the ring take my stalwart horse.
He could bear me once
with speed through the heavens.
With me
he lost this most mighty art.
He will prance no more
through lightning and thunder,
nor soar
daringly over the clouds.
But wherever you lead—
even through fire—
fearlessly Grane will follow.
For you, O hero,
now are his master!
So hold him well,
he'll heed your word.
O, often bring him
fond greetings from me.

SIEGFRIED.

Must I achieve all my deeds
only through virtues you give me?
You select my fights for me,
and my victories come from your will.
I stride the steed you gave me,
beneath your sheltering shield—
so now I'm Siegfried no more,
but only Brunnhilda's arm!

BRUNNHILDA.

O, were your soul also Brunnhilda's.

SIEGFRIED.

Through her alone I have heart.

BRUNNHILDA.

That makes you Siegfried and Brunnhild.

SIEGFRIED.

Where I am, both of us harbor.

BRUNNHILDA.

Is my rock-hall deserted then?

SIEGFRIED.

It makes two into one.

BRUNNHILDA.

O, holy immortals,
noble protectors!
Joy in the sight
of a love such as ours.
Apart—none can divide us.
Divided—never apart.

SIEGFRIED.

Hail, O Brunnhild,
radiant star!

BRUNNHILDA.

Hail, O Siegfried,
conquering light!

SIEGFRIED.

Hail, love full of glory!
Hail, radiant star!
Hail, Brunnhild, hail!

BRUNNHILDA.

Hail, love full of glory!
Hail, conquering light!
Hail, hail, hail, hail!

(Siegfried quickly leads the horse to the rocky descent, while Brunnhilda gazes after him from the height for a long while. From the valley the merry sound of Siegfried's horn is heard.
The curtain falls.)

ACT ONE

FIRST SCENE

The Hall of the Gibichungs on the Rhine

The back is quite open, showing a flat shore down to the river; rocky heights around. Gunther and Gutruna are on a throne, before which is a table with drinking vessels. Hagen is seated before it.

GUNTHER.

Now hark, Hagen,
tell me the truth:
is my throne by the Rhine
helpful to Gibich's fame?

HAGEN.

To know your glory
rouses my envy,
but she, your mother and mine,
Dame Grimhild, gave me to know this.

GUNTHER.

I envy you,
you envy me not!
Though I'm lord and heir,
wisdom is yours alone.
How better end
the strife of half-brothers!
Just to ask you of my fame
is to give your judgment praise.

HAGEN.

The blame must be mine
your fame is not great:
I know of high advantage
that the Gibichung has not yet won.

GUNTHER.

I'll blame you too
unless I'm told.

HAGEN.

The Gibichung race has reached
its ripe and summer bloom:
you, Gunther, still unwed,
you, Gutrun, still no mate.

GUNTHER.

Whom would you have me woo
that we may build our fame?

HAGEN.

A rare woman,
none nobler in the world.
Her seat's a rocky height,
a fire flames round her abode.
The one who breaks through that fire
finds Brunnhild, a maid to woo.

GUNTHER.

And have I the courage for that?

HAGEN.

It is meant to be for one more strong.

GUNTHER.

Who is this valorous man?

HAGEN.

Siegfried, the Volsungen son;
he is the mighty man.
A twin-born pair,
in loving attraction,
Siegmund and Sieglind,
begot a legitimate son,
who has grown to strength in the woods—
this hero Gutrun should wed.

GUTRUNA.

Tell me deeds done by this Siegfried,

that he merits a hero's renown.

HAGEN.

> At hate cavern
> the Nibelung hoard
> was watched by a dragon foe.
> Siegfried closed up
> his terrible maw,
> destroyed him with conquering sword.
> Such an unheard-of deed
> gave wings to the hero's fame.

GUNTHER.

> The Nibelung hoard, they tell me,
> includes some wonderful wealth.

HAGEN.

> The one who best knows its use
> will bend all the world to his will.

GUNTHER.

> And Siegfried won it in war?

HAGEN.

> Now are the Nibelungs his slaves.

GUNTHER.

> Can Brunnhild be won by none else?

HAGEN.

> No one else can stifle the blaze.

GUNTHER.
(rising in displeasure)

> Why waken discord and doubt?
> Why do you stir my mind
> to long for a treasure
> I cannot win?

HAGEN.

> But if Siegfried
> should fetch the bride,
> would not Brunnhild be yours?

GUNTHER.

> What power could get this man
> to woo the bride for me?

HAGEN.

> If Gutrun worked an enchantment
> Siegfried then would be bound.

GUTRUNA.

> You mocker, wicked Hagen!
> How can I work enchantment?
> If he's the greatest
> of men on earth,
> the fairest women on earth
> must surely have had his love.

HAGEN.
(confidentially to Gutruna)

> Recall the drink in the chest,
> and trust in me who won the charm.
> The hero for whom you long
> soon can be bound to your love.
> *(Gunther approaches the table, and listens
> attentively, leaning on it.)*
> Siegfried need only come
> and taste of the magical drink.
> That he'd seen a woman ere you,
> or that one ever came near,
> would wholly pass from his mind.
> Now tell me,
> how like you Hagen's plan?

GUNTHER.
*(has again approached the table and listened attentively, lean-
ing on it.)*

> All praise be to Grimhild,
> for brother wise as this!

GUTRUNA.

> I would love to meet this man.

GUNTHER.

> But how can he be found?
> *(A horn is heard in the distance.)*

HAGEN.

> When he is gaily
> questing for fame,
> the world becomes
> a narrow woods.
> Be sure in his quests he will reach
> even Gibich's strand on the Rhine.

GUNTHER.

Surely I'll welcome him well!
*(Siegfried's horn is again heard in the dis-
tance, but nearer. They listen.)*
The sound comes from the Rhine.

HAGEN.
(goes to the bank, looks up and down the river.)
Within a boat a horse and man.
He blows a rollicking horn!
With a casual stroke,
as from idle hand,
he drives the boat
speedily on.
So practised a hand
when he swings the scull
comes but from him
who has done that deed.
Siegfried it is, surely no other!

GUNTHER.

Will he pass by?

HAGEN.
(making a trumpet of his hands and shouting)
Hoiho! Where to,
you merry man?

SIEGFRIED'S VOICE.
(from the distance, on the river)
To Gibich's mighty offspring.

HAGEN.

I bid you welcome
to Gibich's hall!

        (Siegfried's boat appears.)
This way! Here come ashore!
Hail Siegfried! Valiant man!
*(Gunther comes down and joins Hagen. Sieg-
fried brings his boat to the shore. Hagen
makes it fast with the chain. Siegfried springs
ashore with his horse.)*

SIEGFRIED.

Who is Gibich's son?

(He leans on his horse, remaining quietly standing by the boat. Gutruna gazes at him from her throne in astonishment. Gunther prepares to offer him friendly greetings. All stand fixed in silent mutual contemplation.)

GUNTHER.

Gunther, I, whom you seek.

SIEGFRIED.

Your fame is wide
all round the Rhine.
Now fight with me
or else be my friend!

GUNTHER.

Speak of peace:
you are welcome!

SIEGFRIED.

A place for my horse?

HAGEN.

I'll see to that.

SIEGFRIED.

You called me Siegfried.
When did we meet?

HAGEN.

I knew who you were
just by your strength.

SIEGFRIED.

Take care of my Grane!
You've never held
a horse by the bit
so noble in breed.
(Hagen leads the horse away, and returns immediately. Gunther advances into the hall with Siegfried.)

GUNTHER.

Well, hero, hail with joy
the homestead of my father.
The ground you tread on,
all things you see,
treat as your own from henceforth.
Yours is my birthright,

land and people—
add my limbs to this promise,
myself—all these are yours.

SIEGFRIED.

I offer neither men nor land,
nor father's house and court.
All I own
is my life and limbs;
these I spend as I live.
Just a sword is there,
which I welded.
So I swear by my weapon.
My sword and myself are yours.

HAGEN.

Yet from tales that are told
you won the Nibelung hoard.

SIEGFRIED.

I nearly forgot that store.
What good is an idle wealth?
I let it stay there in its cavern,
where a dragon once kept guard.

HAGEN.

You took no part of it?

SIEGFRIED.
(pointing to the steel network that hangs in his girdle)
Just this piece, which I cannot use.

HAGEN.

The Tarnhelm, truly,
the Nibelungs' wonderful work!
It serves, when set on your head,
to transform you to any shape.
And if you would travel far,
it transports you in a trice.
And was that all that you took?

SIEGFRIED.

Just a ring.

HAGEN.

You're keeping it well?

SIEGFRIED.

A wonderful woman is.

HAGEN.
(aside)

Brunnhilda!

GUNTHER.

I've nothing but toys to give,
even by adding my all.
I will serve you freely, with joy.
*(Hagen has gone to Gutruna's door and now
opens it. Gutruna enters and approaches
Siegfried with a drinking horn.)*

GUTRUNA.

Welcome, O guest,
to Gibich's house!
It's his daughter gives you the drink.

SIEGFRIED.
*(bows pleasantly and takes the horn; he holds it thoughtfully
before him, and says softly.)*

Were all forgot
of what you had given,
one lesson
would stay in my mind.
This first of drinks
to love that's faithful,
Brunnhilda, is to you!
*(He drinks, and hands back the horn to
Gutruna, who, ashamed and confused, casts
down her eyes.)*

SIEGFRIED.
(gazing at her with sudden passion)

You beautiful one,
whose looks fire my heart,
why cast down your eyes before mine?
(Gutruna looks up, blushing.)
Ha, fairest maid!
hide that bright gaze.
The heart in my breast
burns from its beams.
Their fiery force consumes
all the blood that flows in my veins!
(with trembling voice)

Gunther—what name has your sister?

GUNTHER.

Gutruna.

SIEGFRIED.

But are they runes of good
that I read in her glances?
          (*He ardently seizes Gutruna's hand.*)
When I sought to be your brother's man,
the haughty one refused.
Would you be just as arrogant
if I asked you the same?
(*Gutruna humbly droops her head and then,
with deprecating gesture, leaves the hall
          again with trembling steps.*)

SIEGFRIED.
(*closely observed by Hagen and Gunther, gazes after her as if
spellbound. Then, without turning, he asks:*)
Have you, Gunther, a wife?

GUNTHER.

I'm not yet wed,
nor, do I think,
likely to find a wife!
My mind is set though on one,
but advice will not avail.

SIEGFRIED.

But how could you fail
were I to help?

GUNTHER.

She dwells upon a rock;
a fire surrounds her home.

SIEGFRIED.
(*repeating the words, as if trying to remember something
half-forgotten*)
"She dwells upon a rock;
a fire surrounds her home . . . ?"

GUNTHER.

But he who can brave that fire—

SIEGFRIED.

"But he who can brave that fire . . . ?"

GUNTHER.

wins Brunnhilda for his wife.

I dare not attempt the ascension;
the fire won't fade for me.

SIEGFRIED.
(with a sudden start)

I—fear not the fear:
the bride soon shall be yours.
I'm your man, henceforth,
and my strength is yours—
provided that Gutrun is mine.

GUNTHER.

Gladly I'll grant you my sister.

SIEGFRIED.

Soon you'll see Brunnhild here.

GUNTHER.

But how will you fool her?

SIEGFRIED.

Through the Tarnhelm's magic,
which will give me your form.

GUNTHER.

So then an oath must be sworn!

SIEGFRIED.

Blood-brotherhood
hallowed by oath!
*(Hagen fills a drinking horn with wine; he
holds it out to Siegfried and Gunther, who
cut their arms with their swords and hold
them over the horn for a moment; they then
each lay two fingers on the horn, which
Hagen continues to hold between them.)*

SIEGFRIED &
GUNTHER.

Vigorous blood
of flowering life
drops straight into the drink.
Brothers' courage
blends in our oath.
See the glow of our blood.
Troth I drink to my friend!
Glad and free
upspring from our league

blood-brotherhood now!
But if brother in blood
breaks his vow to his friend,
what we two today
hereby are drinking
will gush most bitterly forth,
till requital be made.
So—here's to our league!
So—here's to good faith!
(Gunther drinks and hands the horn to Sieg-
fried, who finishes the draught and holds the
empty horn to Hagen. Hagen breaks the horn
in two with his sword. Gunther and Siegfried
clasp hands.)

SIEGFRIED.
(to Hagen)

Why did you not join in the oath?

HAGEN.

My blood would ruin the drink.
It flows not clear and noble like yours;
sluggish and cold,
scarcely stirs.
My cheeks can hardly be reddened.
It's not for me,
this hot-headed league!

GUNTHER.
(to Siegfried)

Pay no heed to this churl.

SIEGFRIED.

Fresh for the trip,
there lies my skiff.
Quick, on to the mountain.
Wait on shore for one night,
till I arrive there,
and then bear home the bride.
(He starts for the shore.)

GUNTHER.

Will you not first take rest?

SIEGFRIED.

My return trip will be fast.
> (*He beckons Gunther.*)

GUNTHER.

You, Hagen, take care of the homestead!
> (*He follows Siegfried. While Siegfried and Gunther, after putting their swords in the boat, hoist the sail and make ready for departure, Hagen takes up his spear and shield. Gutruna appears at the door of her chamber just as Siegfried pushes out the boat to the middle of the stream.*)

GUTRUNA.

And now, where are they speeding?

HAGEN.
> (*seating himself comfortably before the hall with spear and shield*)

To court Brunnhilda for bride.

GUTRUNA.

Siegfried?

HAGEN.

See how he strives
for you, wanting to win you!
> (*Siegfried and Gunther fare away.*)

GUTRUNA.

Siegfried—mine?
> (*She goes back to her chamber in much emotion.*)

HAGEN.

I sit here and wait,
keeping the house,
guarding the place against foes.
Gibich's son
is blown by the wind,
as off a-wooing he goes.
A mighty hero
is at the helm,
to brave what danger may come.
And down the Rhine
he'll bring his own bride.
But he will bring me—the ring!

You hearty brothers,
merry companions,
sail on your rollicking way!
Though he seems abject,
you yet shall serve
the Nibelung's son.

SECOND SCENE

The Valkyrie's Rock

Brunnhilda is sitting at the mouth of the cave in silent thought. Moved by blissful memories, she covers the ring with kisses. Distant thunder is heard; she looks up and listens. She turns to the ring again. A flash of lightning. Again she listens, and looks into the distance, whence a dark thunder-cloud is moving toward the rock.

BRUNNHILDA.

Once-familiar sounds
near like a rushing tempest.
A horse comes flying
through the air.
He is riding through
the clouds to this rock.
Who seeks the lonely one here?

VALTRAUTA'S VOICE.
(from the distance)

Brunnhilda! Sister!
Wake to my tidings!

(Brunnhilda starts up.)

BRUNNHILDA.

Valtrauta's cry,
so welcome to hear!
Valiant sister,
have you dared to fly here?

((calling)

See the pines.
As oft of old,
get off your steed:
allow the runner a rest.
*(She rushes into the pine woods, from whence
is heard a mighty sound as of a thunderbolt.
She returns, profoundly moved, with Valtrauta. She appears happy, not noticing Valtrauta's anguished countenance.)*
So you have come?
Are you that bold,
daring to seek me,
Brunnhild, banished from home!

VALTRAUTA.

I have come in haste for your sake.

BRUNNHILDA.

Was love for me
cause why you broke
Valfather's stern commandment?
Or what else? O say!
Has Wotan's heart
softened at my plight?
When I sheltered Siegmund,
braving our father,
wrongly—I know it—
I yet fulfilled his desire.
And I knew that his anger
was no more.
For though sealing my eyes in sleep,
binding me fast to this rock,
giving me up to the man
who should find me here and awake me,
yet he heard my prayer,
and quelled my fear,
surrounding my rock
with a terrible fire,
to frighten all cowards away.
So my punishment
turned to a blessing:

the noblest of heroes
won me for wife!
Blest in his love
I bask in light and delight.
(*She embraces Valtrauta joyfully.*)
Were you allured by my fate?
Do you desire
to share in my pleasures,
feast on these joys of mine?

VALTRAUTA.

Share in the tumult
which you foolishly chose?
Another thing drove me in fear
to brave the will of the god.

BRUNNHILDA.

Fear and dread
hold you in terror.
So his wrath has never let up.
You fear his full punishment's force.

VALTRAUTA.

If I could fear him
then my grief soon would be gone.

BRUNNHILDA.

Really, I don't understand.

VALTRAUTA.

Master your emotion:
heed the words I must say.
My terror drives me
back to Valhall,
which from Valhall drove me to you.

BRUNNHILDA.

What's wrong with the gods of the
heavens?

VALTRAUTA.

Heed with your mind what I must tell
you!
Since you and he were parted,
he's never sent us
to the battles.
So we roam,

a wretched and leaderless troop.
As for Valhalla's heroes,
our lord shunned them.
Then, on his steed,
without let or rest,
he wandered alone through the world.
He lately came home,
holding fast in his hand
his spear in splinters.
Some hero had hacked it in pieces.
With silent signs
Wotan sent his men
to the woods,
to fell the mighty ash tree.
He bade them take
the pieces of trunk
and to pile them up high
round the great hall of the blest.
He called the gods
unto a council,
and sacredly
sat there on high.
Then he bade
the terrified ones to sit near him,
In rank and row
the hall was filled with the heroes.
There—sits he,
says no word,
upon his high seat,
still and grave,
the splintered spear
held fast in his hand.
Holda's apples
tempt not at all.
Fear and amazement
make the gods seem frozen.
Then he set both ravens
free for a journey.
If they return

with news that's welcome to hear,
once more only—
a final time—
we will perceive father smile.
Round his knees the Valkyrs
lie at his feet sadly.
Yet Wotan
is deaf to our pleading.
We're burdened by fear,
anguish and endless despair.
Upon his breast
weeping, I sorrowed.
And then he broke down.
And his thoughts were—Brunnhilda—you.
His eyes were closed,
he sighed deeply,
and as if dreaming,
he spoke like this:
"The day the Rhine-king's daughters
get back the ring that once they
     possessed,
marks the curse's end,
and gods and men be free."
I thought on this,
and then I left him,
through silent heroes
stealing away.
I got on my horse
in secretive haste,
and rode the storm to the rock.
Now, O sister,
I beg your help.
Bravely perform
whatever you can.
Cancel the doom of the gods.
    (*She throws herself at Brunnhilda's feet.*)

BRUNNHILDA.

What whirling words are these,
what fearful and nightmarish tales!

I'm just a fool who's been banished
from the holy vapors of heaven:
I cannot grasp what you tell me.
Words like these
seem to me vain.
Within your eyes—
so heavy-weary—
gleams flicker and glow.
Your cheeks are ashen,
O pallid sister,
what wild thing is it you want?

VALTRAUTA.

It's on your hand—the ring—
just that: hear my advice!
For Wotan, cast it from you!

BRUNNHILDA.

The ring—from me?

VALTRAUTA.

The Rhine-daughters own it by rights!

BRUNNHILDA.

The Rhine-daughters—I—the ring?
Siegfried's pledge of love?
Have you gone crazy?

VALTRAUTA.

Hear me! Heed my distress!
The world's troubles
hang right squarely on it.
Cast it from you, right in the water.
End the sorrow of Valhall,
cast the curst thing into the waves.

BRUNNHILDA.

Ha! Think now, what this would mean!
Unfeeling maid,
you do not perceive.
More than Valhall's raptures,
more than the glory of gods,
I count this ring.
A glance of its gleaming gold,
a flash of its noble light
is more precious

to me than is the lasting
luck of all the gods.
For Siegfried's dear love
blesses by shining from it.
Siegfried loves me!
O, might I but tell you the rapture
bound up in the ring!
Get hence to the holy
council of gods!
And of my ring
just tell them this one thing:
I never will renounce love,
nor can they keep me from loving—
rather let Valhall
crash to earth.

VALTRAUTA.   This is your faith, then!
In her trouble
you coldly abandon your sister?

BRUNNHILDA.   Off on your way!
Flee to your horse!
I'll not relinquish the ring!

VALTRAUTA.   Woe's me! Woe's me!
Woe's you, sister!
Gods of Valhall, woe!
*(She rushes away. Soon a stormcloud rises
from the woods with sounds of a tempest, and
quickly sails away into the distance.)*

BRUNNHILDA.   Thundering cloud,
you wind-blown bauble,
be on your way!
Storm hence and never come back!
*(It is now evening. From the valley glimmers
the gradually growing firelight.)*
Shadows of evening
shroud the heavens.
My guardian fires leap up!
The flames are raging,

and licking their tongues to the wall.
The fiery tide
rolls up to the peak of the rock.

(She starts in rapture.)

Siegfried!
Siegfried is back?
It is he sending his call.
Up! Up, to be gathered
into my god's embrace!
*(She hastens joyfully to the edge of the crag.
Flames leap up, out of which Siegfried
springs forward onto a high rock, whereupon
the flames immediately withdraw and again
only shine up from below. Brunnhilda recoils,
flies to the foreground, and from there, in
speechless astonishment, stares at Siegfried,
who has appeared in Gunther's form, wearing the Tarnhelm, whose visor covers half
his face, leaving only the eyes free.)*

BRUNNHILDA.
(retreating in horror)

Betrayed! What man are you?

SIEGFRIED.
*(remaining on the rock, motionless and leaning on his shield as
he gazes at her. He speaks harshly.)*

Brunnhild, your wooer comes,
one who's fearless of the fire.
I've come here for a wife.
So follow where I lead.

BRUNNHILDA.

Who is the man
who has achieved that
which the strongest only can?

SIEGFRIED.

A hero, who'll be tamed
when once you yield your might.

BRUNNHILDA.
(terrified)

A demon's climbed
to this rocky peak.
An eagle has flown here
to tear me to bits!

Who are you, dreadful one?
> *(Siegfried is silent.)*

Are you a human?
Are you of Hella's
hosts of the night?

SIEGFRIED.

A Gibichung am I,
and Gunther is my name,
whom, maid, you'll follow now.

BRUNNHILDA.
(in an outburst of despair)

Wotan! you grim
and terrible god!
Woe! Now I fathom
your wrathful curse!
My shame and sorrow
come from your will!

SIEGFRIED.
(leaping from the rock and approaching)

The night has come,
I ask for your room,
you must be mine for marriage.

BRUNNHILDA.
(threateningly stretching out her finger on which is Siegfried's ring)

Stand back! Flee from this token!
You cannot take me by force,
while yet this ring stands on guard.

SIEGFRIED.

This is a token for Gunther:
he will wed you with this ring.

BRUNNHILDA.

Go back, you robber!
Villainous thief!
Don't venture, you rogue, to come near!
This is my strength,
stronger than steel.
This—cannot be robbed!

SIEGFRIED.

Why then you shall teach me

how it is mine.
*(He presses toward her. They struggle.
Brunnhilda tears herself free and flies. Siegfried pursues her. Again they struggle. He
seizes her and plucks the ring from her finger.
She utters a loud scream and sinks exhausted
on the rocky seat in front of the cave.)*

Now you are mine!
Brunnhilda, Gunther's bride.
Go with me now to your room.

BRUNNHILDA.
(almost fainting)

Most wretched of women,
what help do I have?
*(Siegfried drives her in commandingly. She
goes into the cave, trembling, and with
tottering steps.)*

SIEGFRIED.
(drawing his sword)

Now, Needful, witness here,
that I have chastely wooed,
and kept my oath to my brother.
Serve as wall between us two.
(He follows Brunnhilda.)

Act Two

A River Bank

Before the hall of the Gibichungs: to the right the open entrance to the hall, to the left the bank of the Rhine. From the latter mounting toward the back, rises a rocky height, cut by several mountain paths. There an altar-stone to Fricka is visible, as well as one, higher up, to Wotan, and one at the side to Donner. It is night. Hagen, spear in hand and shield at side, sits sleeping against the hall. The moon suddenly throws a keen light on him and his surroundings: Alberich is seen crouching in front of him, leaning his arms on Hagen's knees.

ALBERICH.
(softly)

> Sleeping, Hagen, my son?
> You sleep and hear not him
> whom rest and sleep forsake?

HAGEN.
(softly and without moving)

> I hear you well, harassed elfin.
> What is it I should know while sleeping?

ALBERICH.

> Remember the might
> you are endowed with—
> if you've the courage
> that your mother gave you at birth.

295

HAGEN.

My courage came from her,
and yet I cannot thank her
that she succumbed to your spell.
Wizened, wan and pale,
I hate the happy,
never rejoice.

ALBERICH.

Hagen, my son,
hate all the happy,
but love as you should
the one who's so sad
and burdened with care.
If you are hardy,
bold and smart,
those whom we strive with
in conflict by night
will soon bear the marks of our spite.
The one who once seized my ring,
Wotan, the ravening robber,
at last has been vanquished
by his own offspring.
Through the Volsung he's lost
his power and might.
With the gods assembled round him
he waits his downfall in anguish.
My fear now has gone:
he will perish among them.
Sleeping, Hagen, my son?

HAGEN.
(still motionless)

Who's heir to the might
of gods above?

ALBERICH.

I—and you:
we're heirs of the world,
if I can count
upon your faith,
sharing both my woe and wrath.
Wotan's spear

was split by the Volsung.
And through his great might
the dragon was slain.
He playfully picked up the ring.
Now he is lord of every power.
Valhall and Nibelhome
bow to his might.
Since this hero is fearless
my curses are lame.
He knows not how the ring is used,
he knows not its murderous might.
Laughter and love fill his heart:
joy in living is his.
Now we must plot
just how to destroy him.
Sleeping, Hagen, my son?

HAGEN.
(as before)

Already I've helped him
toward his doom.

ALBERICH.

The golden ring—
the ring—*that* we must capture.
A cunning, wise woman
lives for his love:
if she advise
that he return it
to the waters where
the Rhine-maidens live—
those girls who made me a fool—
the circlet then will be lost;
and no art will win it again.
Therefore delay not,
aim for the ring.
I bred you
as one without fear,
so you could fight my foes
when I needed.
True, you were not strong

enough for that foe
which the Volsung slaughtered with ease.
I brought up Hagen
to live in hate,
and this son shall avenge me,
and win the circlet—
then Volsung and Wotan are doomed!
Swear to me, Hagen, my son?

HAGEN.
(An increasing shadow covers Alberich while day begins to dawn.)

The ring shall be ravished:
rest now in peace.

ALBERICH.

Swear to me, Hagen, my son?

HAGEN.

My heart swears it.
Silence your sorrow.
(An increasing gloom hides Hagen and Alber-
ich. Day is arriving on the Rhine.)

ALBERICH.
(his voice fainter and fainter)

Be true, Hagen, my son,
trusty hero, be true.
Be true—true!
(He vanishes completely. Hagen stares fixedly
upon the Rhine. The sun rises and is mirrored
in the waters. Suddenly Siegfried comes for-
ward from behind a bush on the river bank.
He bears his own form, but the Tarnhelm is
still on his head. He takes this off as he ad-
vances, and hangs it on his girdle.)

SIEGFRIED.

Hoiho! Hagen!
Weary man!
How did I get here?

HAGEN.
(rising indolently)

Hey! Siegfried!
Most speedy hero!
Where were you till now?

SIEGFRIED.

> At Brunnhilda's rock;
> and there I drew in that breath
> I spent when I called:
> so fast was my exploit.
> Two that are coming, must lag.
> A boat now bears them here.

HAGEN.

> You mastered Brunnhild?

SIEGFRIED.

> Where's Gutruna?

HAGEN.
(calling toward the hall)

> Hoiho! Gutruna!
> Come on out!
> Siegfried is here;
> why stay inside?

SIEGFRIED.
(turning toward the hall)

> I'll tell you both
> the way I bound Brunnhild.
> *(Gutruna approaches him from the hall.)*
> Now bid me welcome,
> Gibich child.
> I come to you with happy news.

GUTRUNA.

> Freia give you joy,
> to every woman's honor!

SIEGFRIED.

> Freely grant me
> joy and favor!
> This day has made you my wife.

GUTRUNA.

> Does Brunnhild come with my brother?

SIEGFRIED.

> Soon did he win what he wished.

GUTRUNA.

> Was he not singed by the fire?

SIEGFRIED.

> No, it would not have done harm,

and yet I stepped through for him,
to win the prize of Gutrun!

GUTRUNA.

You went right through unscathed?

SIEGFRIED.

The flickering fire was fun!

GUTRUNA.

Did Brunnhild think you Gunther?

SIEGFRIED.

We looked as like as hairs.
The Tarnhelm did the trick,
as Hagen told me it would.

HAGEN.

I gave you good advice.

GUTRUNA.

You mastered the valiant maid?

SIEGFRIED.

She felt—Gunther's might.

GUTRUNA.

Was she married then to you?

SIEGFRIED.

She obeyed her rightful husband
for a full and marital night.

GUTRUNA.

Did you pass as rightful spouse?

SIEGFRIED.

The one I await is Gutrun.

GUTRUNA.

Yet did Brunnhild lie beside him?

SIEGFRIED.

East and West are near the North;
So near was Brunnhild, so far.

GUTRUNA.

How then did Gunther obtain the bride?

SIEGFRIED.

Through the flames that were flickering
     and dying,
Through morn's mists from the rock
she followed me down the vale.
And near the shore

I and Gunther
made exchange of our forms:
Then, through the helmet's virtue,
flash, I am straightway here.
A driving wind now brings
the dear ones right up the Rhine.
So greet them well when they come!

GUTRUNA.

Siegfried, masterful man,
I feel afraid of you!

HAGEN.
(calling from the shore)
I can see a sail in the distance!

SIEGFRIED.

So give the herald thanks!

GUTRUNA.

Let her have a gracious welcome
to please her so she'll love to tarry.
You Hagen! gaily
summon the vassals
to Gibich's court for wedding,
while I call the maids to the feast.
They'll merrily join in the fun!
*(As she goes toward the hall she turns round
again.)*
Man of war, won't you rest?

SIEGFRIED

Just to help you gives me rest.
(He follows her. Both go into the hall.)

HAGEN.
(standing on a rock at the back, starts blowing his cow-horn)
Hoiho! Hoiho! Hoiho!
You men of Gibich!
Get yourselves up!
Waken! Waken!
Weapons! Weapons!
Arm through the land!
Goodly weapons!
Mighty weapons!
Sharp for strife!

Foes are here!
Foes! Waken!
Hoiho! Hoihohoho!
*(Hagen remains on his station. Other horns
answer his from different directions. From
the heights and valleys armed men rush on.)*

THE VASSALS.
(a few first, then gradually increasing in number)

Why blares the horn?
What calls us to war?
We come with our arms,
we come with our weapons,
with mighty weapons,
with keenest arms!
Hoiho! Hoiho!
Hagen! Hagen!
What's the danger here?
Who's the foe that's near?
Who comes to fight?
Is Gunther in need?

HAGEN.

Ready yourselves
and waste no time.
Gunther soon will be here.
Your lord comes with a bride.

THE MEN.

What is his need?
Who is it threats?

HAGEN.

He's bringing a wife
fiery and proud.

THE MEN.

Do furious kinsfolk
follow for vengeance?

HAGEN.

No one follows.
He's alone.

THE MEN.

Has he righted a wrong
and conquered in war?

Tell us now.

HAGEN.

The dragon-destroyer gave aid:
Siegfried the brave gave mighty help!

THE MEN.

Then what is the need of our army?

HAGEN.

Steers of value
must be slaughtered,
and Wotan's altar
must flow with their blood.

THE MEN.

Why, Hagen, what would you have us do?

HAGEN.

Let a boar be slaughtered:
Thus honor Froh.
Get a vigorous goat,
slay it for Donner.
Sheep must then be
slaughtered for Fricka,
to gain her blessing in wedlock.

THE MEN.
(with ever increasing mirth)

When we have slain them,
what then shall we do?

HAGEN.

You'll take the cup
from lovely maids,
and down the drinks
of mead and of wine!

THE MEN.

The cup in our hands,
what then are we to do?

HAGEN.

Revel away
till your wits are wet.
Thus you will honor the gods
and they will then prosper the marriage!

THE MEN.
(with ringing peals of laughter)

> Great luck now smiles
> here on the Rhine,
> when Hagen, the grim one,
> indulges in mirth!
> The prickly thorn
> prickles no more!
> A wedding-helper
> let him be called!

HAGEN.
(quite serious)

> Now leave off laughing,
> valiant vassals!
> Receive Gunther's bride:
> Brunnhilda nears now with him.
> *(He descends and joins the men. He orders*
> *them toward the Rhine. Some hasten to the*
> *heights, others to the banks.)*
> Honor your mistress,
> pledge her your truth;
> if she is wronged
> haste to avenge her.
> *(Gunther and Brunnhilda arrive in the boat.*
> *Some of the men spring into the water and*
> *drag the boat ashore. While Gunther con-*
> *ducts Brunnhilda ashore, the men shout and*
> *clash their weapons. Hagen stands off.)*

THE MEN.

> Hail! Hail!
> We greet you! Be welcome!
> Hail, O Gunther!
> Hail to your bride!

GUNTHER.
(presenting Brunnhilda, who follows him with pale and down-cast looks.)

> Brunnhild, most queenly bride
> comes with me to our shores.
> No man ever won
> a nobler woman.

The Gibichungs' lofty race
received the favor of gods.
Their highest fame
now has arrived.

THE MEN.

Hail! Hail to you, Gunther!
Fortunate Gibichung!
*(Gunther leads Brunnhilda toward the hall,
from which Siegfried and Gutruna, attended
by women, step forth.)*

GUNTHER.

All hail, most valiant man!
All hail, lovely sister!
I joy to see you beside him
who won you for his bride.
Two blessed couples,
glowing and radiant,
Brunnhilda—and Gunther,
Gutruna—and Siegfried!
*(Brunnhilda, startled, raises her eyes and per-
ceives Siegfried. She drops Gunther's hand,
steps toward Siegfried, then recoils in horror
and glares at him. All are wonder-struck.)*

MEN & WOMAN.

What ails her?
Is she distraught?

SIEGFRIED.

What clouds Brunnhilda's look?

BRUNNHILDA.
(almost swooning)

Siegfried . . . here. . . ! Gutruna. . . ?

SIEGFRIED.

Gunther's gentle sister.
She's my bride,
as you are his.

BRUNNHILDA.

I . . . Gunther. . . ? You lie!
The light has gone out!
(She nearly falls. Siegfried supports her.)
Siegfried . . . knows me not!

SIEGFRIED.

> Gunther, see, your wife is ailing!
>> *(Gunther steps over to her.)*
>
> Awaken, wife,
> here is your husband!
> *(As Siegfried points to Gunther, Brunnhilda*
>> *perceives the ring on his finger.)*

BRUNNHILDA.
(with a fearful start)

> Ha—the ring
> upon his hand.
> He . . . Siegfried?

MEN & WOMEN.

> What's wrong?

HAGEN.
(advancing)

> Now listen well
> to the woman's plaint.

BRUNNHILDA.
(trying to control her emotion)

> On your hand there
> I beheld a ring:
> you do now own it,
> it was ravished—
>> *(pointing to Gunther)*
>
> by this man.
> But how did the ring
> come into your hands?

SIEGFRIED.
(attentively studying the ring on his finger)

> This ring—it did not
> come from him.

BRUNNHILDA.
(to Gunther)

> If it was you who seized
> this ring that made us one,
> assert your rightful claim:
> get back your pledge again.

GUNTHER.
(perplexed)

> The ring—I did not give it.

You, though, must know him well.

BRUNNHILDA.

Where have you kept the ring
that I was forced to give you?
> *(Gunther, bewildered, remains silent.)*
Ha! Here's the man!
This is he who took my ring:
Siegfried, the treacherous thief!

SIEGFRIED.
(absorbed in contemplation of the ring)

No woman, sure,
gave me this ring,
nor was it torn
from off a woman's hand.
I know it well
as a prize of strife
which I won at hate-cavern once
when I slew the dragon on guard.

HAGEN.
(stepping between them)

Brunnhild, valiant wife!
Say if you know this ring.
If you gave it to your spouse,
then it is his,
and Siegfried obtained it through guile,
and the traitor must pay for the theft.

BRUNNHILDA.
(shrieking in anguish)

Deceit! Deceit!
Dastardly deceit!
Betrayed; Betrayed!
Wrong too black for revenge!

GUTRUNA.

Deceit?

MEN & WOMEN.

But who's betrayed?

BRUNNHILDA.

Gods immortal!
Heavenly leaders!
Did your decrees

include such woe?
Grief you have taught me
as none ever knew,
painfullest shame
unfelt till this hour!
Grant me such vengeance
as never was known!
Kindle a wrath
that can never be quenched!
Order Brunnhild's
poor heart to be shattered,
if he who wronged her
may be destroyed!

GUNTHER.

Brunnhild, beloved,
calm yourself!

BRUNNHILDA.

Away, betrayer!
Yes—betrayed one!
All of you, listen!
Not he—
but—that one there—
he is my spouse.

MEN & WOMEN.

Siegfried? Gutruna's spouse?

BRUNNHILDA.

He forced delight
and love from me.

SIEGFRIED.

Are you so careless
of your honor?
The tongue then—that condemns you—
must I accuse it of lying?
Hear, if I broke my faith!
Blood-brotherhood
was my promise to Gunther,
Needful, my trusty sword,
guarded the solemn oath;
its sharpness stood as barrier
against this wretched bride.

BRUNNHILDA.

You hero in fraud,
look how you lie!
Why do you vainly
swear by your sword!
I know quite well its sharpness,
and also the scabbard,
within which, snugly
slept on the wall,
Needful, that loyal friend,
while his master paid court to his bride.

THE MEN.
(crowding together, angrily)

What, did he turn traitor,
sullying Gunther's honor?

GUNTHER.

My shame is heavy,
void of defense,
if you don't answer
what she has said.

GUTRUNA.

Faithless, Siegfried?
Are you untrue?
Attest that the tale
she tells is false.

THE MEN.

Clear yourself now,
if you are true.
Silence her clamors!
Swear with an oath!

SIEGFRIED.

Silence her clamors?
Swear with an oath?
Which of you men here
will lend me his arms?

HAGEN.

I have here my spear-point:

that I will lend.
It guards the honor of oaths.
(The men form a ring round Siegfried and Hagen. The latter extends the spear. Siegfried lays two fingers of his right hand upon the point.)

SIEGFRIED.

Shining spear!
Hallowed weapon!
Come to the aid of my honor!
By this shining spear-point
Here is my oath:
Spear-point, hark to my words!
If sharpness can pierce me,
yours be the point;
and if death must attack me,
yours be the blow—
if I have wronged this bride,
if I have frauded my friend.

BRUNNHILDA.
(enters the circle wrathfully, thrusts Siegfried's hand from the spear and touches the point with her own.)

Shining spear!
Hallowed weapon!
Come to the aid of my honor!
By this shining spear-point
here is my oath:
spear-point, hark to my words!
I consecrate your weight
to his undoing!
and I bless this keen-edged blade
for his destruction!
He stands here a traitor to vows,
perfidious! Fraud is his name!

THE MEN.
(in an uproar)

Help, Donner!
bring on your thunder
to silence this roaring disgrace!

SIEGFRIED.

Gunther, look to this woman,
whose shameless words bring you shame!
Give her time and rest,
this untamed mountain maid,
until that shrewish rage is quiet,
which by some demon's
artful spite
rouses confusion in all!
You vassals, be on your way.
None but women should scold!
We're cowards, what are we else,
using as weapons our tongues!

(advancing to Gunther)

I'm more annoyed than you
I played my part so ill.
The Tarnhelm, I suspect,
was but a half disguise.
Yet woman's wrath
quickly abates:
she will then rejoice,
thankful I won her for you.

(turning again to the men)

Frolic, good fellows,
come to the feast!
To the wedding, maidens,
make merry!
Joy as you please,
laugh as you will.
In court and grove,
first in the frolic,
watch me revel it up!
You who live and love,
let my jolly spirits
move you to join in my mirth!

*(Zestfully he puts his arm around Gutruna
and draws her into the hall with him. The
men and women follow. Brunnhilda, Gunther
and Hagen remain behind. Gunther, in deep
shame and dejection, with face covered, has*

*seated himself on one side. Brunnhilda gazes
for a time sorrowfully after Siegfried and
Gutruna, then drops her head.)*

BRUNNHILDA.

Does some devil's plot
lie here in hiding?
Has a wizard's will
brought on this woe?
Where is now my wisdom
'gainst this confusion?
And where are the runes
I need for this riddle?
Ah, sorrow, sorrow!
Woe! Ah, woe!
I gave all my
wisdom to him!
He holds the maid
fast in his power.
I am in bondage,
held as his booty,
whom, weeping—though in despite—
lightly the hero casts off!
Who'll offer me now the sword
with which I may sever my bonds?

HAGEN.
(*approaching*)

Just trust in me,
offended wife!
I'll right your wrongs
and wreak revenge!

BRUNNHILDA.

On whom?

HAGEN.

On Siegfried, treacherous cheat!

BRUNNHILDA.

On Siegfried? You?
                (*She laughs bitterly.*
One single glance
of his eyes as they lighten—
which even disguise could not hide,

when they dazzled my sight—
would lay low
your most valorous spirits!

HAGEN.

Why should his falsehood
spare him from vengeance?

BRUNNHILDA.

Truth, and falsehood—
wearisome words!
Seek stronger means
to enforce your weapon,
if you would slay the most strong!

HAGEN.

I know his conquering
power quite well.
It's hard to vanquish this hero.
So whisper to me
a cunning spell
to make this warrior weak.

BRUNNHILDA.

O thankless! Shameful return!
All of the arts
within my lore
were employed to guard Siegfried's life.
Yet he knows not
of my magic spells
that keep him free from every wound.

HAGEN.

You mean there's no blade can hurt him?

BRUNNHILDA.

In battle, no—yet—
if you can strike his back . . .
Never—I know this—
would he retreat.
He never showed his back to foemen.
So there I spared my protection.

HAGEN.

My spear knows where to strike.
              (*He turns to Gunther.*
Up, Gunther!

Noble Gibichung!
Here stands your valiant wife.
Why hang around and mope?

GUNTHER.
(rising sorrowfully)

O shame!
Dishonor!
Woe is me,
most sorrowful of mortals!

HAGEN.

Your shame is mighty,
who can doubt?

BRUNNHILDA.

O craven man!
Treacherous mate!
Hiding behind
the hero you crouched,
awaiting the prize
from him who was victor!
Low indeed
our race must have sunk
to bear a dastard like you!

GUNTHER.
(beside himself)

Deceived I—and deceived one!
Betrayer I—and betrayed one!
I'm crushed to the core,
and pierced to the heart!
Help, Hagen!
Help save my honor!
Help for your mother!
For you, too, are her son!

HAGEN.

No brain can help,
no hand can give aid.
Your help is—Siegfried's death!

GUNTHER.

Siegfried's death!

HAGEN.

Just this wipes out your shame!

GUNTHER.
(staring horror-struck)

> Blood-brotherhood
> made us as one!

HAGEN.

> The broken bond
> calls for his blood!

GUNTHER.

> Was he untrue?

BRUNNHILDA.

> He betrayed you,
> and all have wrought my betrayal!
> Were I avenged,
> all the blood on earth
> would not suffice for your crime!
> Yet the death of one
> fulfills all justice:
> Siegfried's downfall
> pays sins of his own—and yours!

HAGEN.
(turning to Gunther)

> His downfall—brings you gain.
> Power unheard of will be yours
> if you can win but the ring,
> which his death alone can achieve.

GUNTHER.
(softly)

> Brunnhilda's ring?

HAGEN.

> The Nibelungen ring.

GUNTHER.
(sighing deeply)

> Must this be Siegfried's downfall?

HAGEN.

> His death will help us all.

GUNTHER.

> But, Gutruna, ah,
> to whom I gave him!
> If we destroyed her husband
> could we stand before her face?

BRUNNHILDA.
(furiously)

What good was my wisdom?
What use was my cunning?
My helpless despair
makes all things now clear!
Gutruna is the magic
that bewitched my lord away!
Woe strike her down!

HAGEN.
(to Gunther)

Since his death may afflict her,
we must conceal the truth.
We'll go a-hunting
early tomorrow.
Our man will rush on ahead—
we'll find him gored by a boar.

GUNTHER &
BRUNNHILDA.

So shall it be!
Doomed is Siegfried!
Let him now pay
dear for my shame!
He played false
with vows that he swore to:
so let his blood
pay for his guilt!
All-knowing
god of revenge!
All-witnessing
lord of vows!
Wotan! Wotan!
Come to our aid!
Bring on your holy,
terrible troops
hither to hearken
to vengeful vows!

HAGEN.

So shall it be!
Doomed is Siegfried!

Thus let him die,
Thus let him die,
that radiant heart!
Mine is the hoard,
I rightfully own it.
So let it be
taken from him!
Elfin-father!
You fallen prince!
Night-guardian!
Nibelung's lord!
Alberich! Alberich!
Come to my aid!
Summon the Nibelungs
and warn them anew
you are their leader,
the ring's true lord!

*As Gunther and Brunnhilda turn toward the hall they are
met by the outcoming bridal procession. Siegfried, wearing a
wreath of oak leaves, and Gutruna, crowned with flowers, meet
them at the entrance. Gunther grasps Brunnhilda by the hand
and follows with her. Hagen alone remains behind.*

ACT THREE

A Wild, Woody and Rocky Valley

The Rhine flows past the back by a steep cliff. The three Rhine-daughters, Voglinda, Vellgunda and Flosshilda, rise to the surface of the water and swim around as if in a dance, as they sing the following song.

THE THREE
RHINE-MAIDENS.

O sun-god,
send your rays of glory.
Night lies on the waters.
Once they were bright,
when, fair and clear
our father's gold
lit up their darkness.
Rhinegold!
Gleaming gold!
how bright was once your radiance,
noble star of waters!
Weialala, weialala,
leia, leia, walalala,
leila la la, leila la la.

O Sun-god,
send to us the hero
who will give us back our treasure.
If it were ours,
we nevermore
would envy your eye for its radiance.
Rhinegold!
Gleaming gold!
How glad was your radiance,
noble star of waters!
(Siegfried's horn is heard from the heights.)

VOGLINDA.

The sound of his horn!

VELLGUNDA.

The hero comes.

FLOSSHILDA.

Let us take counsel.
(They all dive down quickly. Siegfried appears on the cliff in full armor.)

SIEGFRIED.

An elfin led me astray,
and so I'm lost on my way.
Hey, rogue! What mountain land
has served for concealing my game?

RHINE-MAIDENS.
(rising again)

Siegfried!

FLOSSHILDA.

But why scold so at the ground?

VELLGUNDA.

Who's the elfin that you blame?

VOGLINDA.

Is it a nixie that nicks?

ALL THREE.

Tell us, Siegfried, speak to us!

SIEGFRIED.
(smilingly)

Did you entice that shaggy
comrade who has

got away from my hands?
If he's your sweetheart,
you're welcome to keep him,
frolicsome maids.

(They laugh aloud.)

VOGLINDA.

Siegfried, what will you give,
if we return your quarry?

SIEGFRIED.

Still am I bootyless,
but tell me what you desire.

VELLGUNDA.

A golden ring
juts on your finger—

ALL THREE
MAIDENS.

We'd like it!

SIEGFRIED.

But to win that ring
I slew a dragon foe.
Why should I let you have it
for the paws of a measly bear?

VOGLINDA.

Stingy indeed!

VELLGUNDA.

So higgling in deals!

FLOSSHILDA.

Free-givers
please the women the best.

SIEGFRIED.

My wife would become quite mad
if I were to waste my goods.

FLOSSHILDA.

Is she that strict?

VELLGUNDA.

She beats you then?

VOGLINDA.

He has often felt her hand!

(They laugh.)

SIEGFRIED.

Enjoy your merry laugh!
I'll still leave you in grief:
don't hope for your desire,
I'll never give you the ring!

FLOSSHILDA.

So fair!

VELLGUNDA.

So strong!

VOGLINDA.

So meet for love!

ALL THREE
MAIDENS.

What pity he's a stingy man!
(They laugh and dive down. Siegfried descends nearer the ground.)

SIEGFRIED.

Why should I bear
this mean report?
Must I thus be shamed?
If they would come
near the shore again,
the fair nixies could have it.
Hey, hey, you merry
water-beauties!
Come quick! I'll give you the ring!
(He takes it from his hands and holds it up. The Rhine-maidens dive up again, now solemn and grave.)

ALL THREE
MAIDENS.

Hold on to it
and guard it well,
until the bad luck is known
that lives within the ring.
Then you will be glad
if we can cancel its curse.

SIEGFRIED.
(quietly putting the ring on his finger again)
Then sing me what you know.

THE RHINE-MAIDENS.

> Siegfried! Siegfried! Siegfried!
> Sorrow lies in your way!
> Let go the ring
> or else you are doomed.
> It was made of gold
> from the river Rhine.
> He who cunningly forged it,
> and lost it in shame,
> put a curse on it,
> to farthest time,
> to bring to his death
> each of its lords.
> As you slew the dragon
> you shall be slain,
> and on this day—
> we tell you this now—
> if you deny us the ring
> which we would hide in the **Rhine-deeps.**
> Only the waves
> cancel the curse!

SIEGFRIED.

> You women of cunning,
> let it be!
> I'm not moved by your flattery,
> and alarms are still less disturbing!

THE RHINE-MAIDENS.

> Siegfried! Siegfried!
> We tell you the truth!
> Yield it! Turn from the curse!
> It makes a strand
> once set by the weavers
> in the cord
> of primal law.

SIEGFRIED.

> My sword once shattered a spear.
> And if the Norns
> have woven this strand,
> putting a curse

in destiny's cord,
Needful shall sunder the weaving.
The dragon once warned me
of this same curse,
yet he never taught me to fear!
The ring granted me
lordship of the earth,
yet the grace of love
buys it from me.
You'd have it too,
just for your love.
But your threat to my life and my limbs
means not as much
as a finger's worth.
You'll never gain the ring thus.
My life and my limbs—see—
*(Here he picks up a clod of earth, holds it
aloft, and at these words throws it behind
him.)*

so—that's what I think of them!

THE RHINE-MAIDENS.

Come, sisters,
Fly from this numbskull!
He fancies himself
so strong and so wise,
but he's fettered and utterly blind!
He has sworn oaths,
and heeded them not!
Runes were given,
he used them not!
A worthy good
was once his prize:
he cast it from him
unawares.
But the ring, which will bring him death,
that ring he wants to hold on to!
Farewell, Siegfried!
A noble wife will today
inherit your token,

She'll listen better than you.
To her! To her! To her!
(They swim away singing. Siegfried looks
after them, smiling.)

SIEGFRIED.

In water, as on the land,
I've learned a lot of woman's wiles:
When all their cajolings fail
they bear one down with threatenings;
and if these fail to work
they lash him with scolding words!
And yet—
were I not Gutrun's spouse,
a girl as fair as these
would suit me well—once she's tamed!
(He gazes after them. Horns are heard ap-
proaching. Siegfried answers gaily on his own
horn. Gunther, Hagen and the men come
down the hills during the following.)

HAGEN.
(His voice is still in the distance.)
Hoiho!

SIEGFRIED.
Hoiho!

THE MEN.
Hoiho! Hoiho!

HAGEN.
(descending from the height, followed by Gunther)
Finally we find you!
Where were you hidden?

SIEGFRIED.
Come on down!
Here it's fresh and cool!
(The men appear on the cliff and follow
down after Hagen and Gunther.)

HAGEN.
We'll rest right here,
and fix up the meal!
(They lay the game in a heap.)
Set down the booty

and offer the wineskins.
(Wineskins and drinking horns are produced.
All lie down.)

You scared away the quarry,
but let us hear of wonders
that Siegfried's gained in hunt!

SIEGFRIED.
(laughing)

Bad—nothing I can eat!
I must depend on you
if I'm to dine.

HAGEN.

No game at all?

SIEGFRIED.

I went on through the woods,
but only found waterfowl there:
had I only reckoned rightly,
I would have captured three
fair birds were in the water,
who sang from the Rhine a warning
that I should die today.
(Gunther starts, and looks gloomily at Hagen.)

HAGEN.

A grievous, fearful hunt,
if a lurking beast should slay
the empty-handed hunter!

SIEGFRIED.

I'm thirsty!
(He has seated himself between Hagen and
Gunther.)

HAGEN.
(filling a drinking-horn and handing it to him)

I've heard it told me, Siegfried,
you understand the meanings
of birds when they sing.
But can this be so?

SIEGFRIED.

It's ages now
since I heeded their chirps.
(He drinks and hands the horn to Gunther.)

Drink, Gunther, drink!
Your brother brings the cup!

GUNTHER.
(gazing into the horn with horror)

The wine is thin and pale:
your blood alone is here!

SIEGFRIED.
(laughing)

Then mingle *your* blood with it.
(He pours from Gunther's horn into his own,
so that it runs over.)
The cup is overflowing.
Why, here's an offering
outpoured to Mother Earth!

GUNTHER.
(sighing)   You overcheerful man!

SIEGFRIED.
(softly to Hagen)

Perhaps Brunnhild has frowned?

HAGEN.

He cannot read her mind
the way you do with birds.

SIEGFRIED.

Since hearing the songs of women
my mind has forgot the birds.

HAGEN.

Yet once you knew them well?

SIEGFRIED.

Hey! Gunther!
Gloomy-faced man!
If I am thanked,
I'll sing you some tales
of the time I was a youngster.

GUNTHER.

I'll listen well.
(All gather near Siegfried, who alone sits
upright, while the others recline.)

HAGEN.   Well hero; sing!

SIEGFRIED.

Mime was
a surly, old dwarf,

who, enforced by need,
brought me up well,
just so this child
when manly enough
could destroy a dragon foe
who long had brooded on a hoard.
He taught me my smithing,
and metal smelting;
but what this craftsman
could not perform,
apprentice zeal
achieved through daring—
forging from steel some broken pieces,
thus remaking a sword.
My father's blade,
fit for the fight,
gleamed in strength.
Needful, I named it.
Now I could fight,
Mime declared,
and led me straight to the wood.
I slew the dragon that day.
Hark, and attend
well to my tale.
How you will hear a wonder:
when some dragon's blood
splashed on to my finger
I brought the burn to my mouth.
I'd hardly moistened the place with my
    tongue
when straight the birds were singing
with words that I could hear!
On a branch he sat there and sang:
"Hey, Siegfried now owns
the Nibelung hoard:
O, let him but find it
within the cave!
Let him but master the Tarnhelm,
'twill serve him for glorious deeds;

but if he could master the ring,
it would make him the lord of the world!"

HAGEN.

Did you bear off
helmet and ring?

THE MEN.

What further came from the birdling?

SIEGFRIED.

Yes, I took
both helmet and ring,
then harked again
to the wonderful warbler,
who sat above me and sang:
"Hey, Siegfried now owns
all the Nibelung hoard,
O, let him not trust
in the treacherous dwarf!
He wants to get hold of the treasure.
Take care, for he's lying in wait!
He is seeking now how to slay you.
So trust not Mime, O Siegfried!"

HAGEN.

How well did he warn?

THE MEN.

What happened with Mime?

SIEGFRIED.

He stepped up to me
with poisonous drink.
Pale and stammering,
the rogue stood before me.
Needful stretched him out quick!

HAGEN.
(*laughing*)

Unable to forge it,
yet he could taste it!
(*He has another drinking-horn filled, and
drops the juice of an herb into it.*)

THE MEN.

And had the bird more to tell you?

HAGEN.
(offering the horn to Siegfried, who looks into it thoughtfully and then drinks slowly)

> Drink first, man,
> from out my horn:
> I brewed you a special drink
> which will waken and brighten your
>   memories,
> so none of the past escapes you.

SIEGFRIED.

> Once more I looked up
> and heard the bird,
> for still he sat and sang—
> "Hey, Siegfried has struck down
> the wicked dwarf!
> Now soon he may take
> a wonderful wife,
> who sleeps surrounded by fire,
> high up on a mountain of rock.
> Who steps through the fire
> wakens the bride:
> Brunnhilda then may be his!"
> *(Gunther listens with increasing astonish-*
> *ment.)*

HAGEN.

> And did you take the birdling's counsel?

SIEGFRIED.

> Off did I go, I never delayed,
> till I came to the fiery rock.
> I stepped through fires
> and found my prize—
> sleeping—a heavenly maid.
> She shone in armor of war.
> I loosened the helmet she wore.
> My kiss awakened the maid.
> Then how burningly the lovely
> Brunnhild embraced me!

GUNTHER.
(springing up in terror)

> What *is* this?

(Two ravens fly out of a bush, circle above Siegfried, and then fly away toward the Rhine.)

HAGEN.

Perhaps you know
What those ravens have said?

(Siegfried starts up suddenly, and turning his back to Hagen, looks after the ravens.)

HAGEN.

Vengeance—such as they asked!

(With these words Hagen thrusts his spear into Siegfried's back. Gunther catches his arm too late.)

GUNTHER & THE MEN.

What have you done here?
What have you done?
(Siegfried swings his shield aloft with both hands in order to throw it on Hagen; his strength fails him; the shield falls back, and he himself falls back upon it.)

HAGEN.
(pointing to the prostrate Siegfried)

Paid the perjured!
(He turns coolly away and gradually disappears over the height, where his retreating form is for some time visible. The anguished Gunther bends over Siegfried. The men stand around the dying man, full of sympathy. Siegfried, supported by two men in a sitting posture, opens radiant eyes.)

SIEGFRIED.

Brunnhilda!
Open your eyes!
Wake up! Heavenly woman!
Are you bound
and fettered in sleep?
Who sealed you in slumber like this?
The wakener came:
his kiss aroused!

He frees her—his bride!
breaking her fetters!
The radiant Brunnhilda smiles!
See her eyes now,
open forever!
Ah, that most blissful
breath of my dear one!
Sweet is my passing,
glorious this shuddering!
Brunnhild cries to me—hail!
*(He sinks back and dies. All manifest grief.
Night has fallen. At Gunther's gesture the
vassals raise Siegfried's body and bear it away
slowly in a solemn procession over the rocky
heights. The moon breaks through the clouds
and lights the procession with increasing
clearness. A mist rises from the Rhine which
gradually fills the atmosphere, at which the
funeral procession becomes invisible. After a
musical interlude the mist parts again until
the hall of the Gibichungs, as in Act I, appears distinctly. Gutruna comes out of her
chamber into the hall.)*

GUTRUNA.

Was that his horn?

(She listens.)

No! He's not yet returned.
I was troubled
by some evil dreams.
Wild whinnies
came from his steed.
Brunnhild's laughter
awaked me from sleep.
I thought I saw
a woman step down to the shore.
I fear this Brunnhild!
Is she at home?
         (She listens at the door and calls.)
Brunnhild! Brunnhild!
Are you up?

*(She opens the door tremblingly and looks
into the inner room.)*

She is not here.
So was it she
I saw go down upon the shore?
Was that his horn?
No! All silent!
If he only were here!

HAGEN'S VOICE.
(from outside)

Hoiho! Hoiho!
Wake up! Wake up!
Torches! Torches!
Torches! Light your torches!
Good game
is here from the hunt!
Hoiho! Hoiho!
*(Lights and increasing glow of fires outside.
Hagen enters the hall.)*

Up! Gutrun,
and greet your Siegfried!
The mighty hero
is coming home!
*(Men and women with torches usher in, in
great agitation, the train with Siegfried's
body. Gunther is among them.)*

GUNTHER.
(terrified)

What is this, Hagen?
I heard not his horn.

HAGEN.

Your pallid man
will blow it no more.
He'll nevermore hie
to hunt or the fight,
nor look for the love of the ladies.

GUTRUNA.
*(with increasing dread as the men set down the body on a
hastily erected bier)*

What do they bring?

HAGEN.

> See, a savage boar has slain him—
> Siegfried—see, your man is dead!

> *(Gutruna shrieks and falls senseless on the
> body. General terror and grief. Gunther at-
> tends to his fainting sister.)*

GUNTHER.

> Gutrun, lovely sister,
> do not be downcast!
> Don't remain mute!

GUTRUNA.
(coming to)

> Siegfried! Siegfried was murdered!
> *(She repels Gunther.)*
> Hence, treacherous brother!
> You murderer of my husband!
> O help me! Help me!
> Horror! Horror!
> They all have murdered my Siegfried!

GUNTHER.

> Don't put the blame on me,
> but put it on to Hagen.
> For he is the boar I spoke of,
> who gored the hero to death.

HAGEN.
(casually)

> So, are you mad at me?

GUNTHER.

> Wrath and misery
> rack you forever!

HAGEN.
(stepping forward in strong defiance)

> Well then! Yes, I was his slayer.
> I, Hagen, dealt him his death!
> And my spear avenged, for on it
> he swore perjury.
> Now, as my sacred prize—
> since I have rightly won it—
> I lay my claim here to the ring.

GUNTHER.

> Keep back! You'll never get

what I declare is mine.

HAGEN.

You vassals, speak for my rights!

GUNTHER.

So you want Gutruna's dowry,
shameless and greedy elf!

HAGEN.
(*drawing his sword*)

The elf will seize it,
for it's his by right!

(*He rushes upon Gunther, who defends himself. They fight. The vassals throw themselves between the two. Gunther is struck by Hagen and falls dead.*)

(*Gutruna screams.*)

Now the ring!
(*Hagen seizes at Siegfried's hand, which raises itself threateningly aloft. All remain spellbound with horror. At this moment Brunnhilda enters solemnly from the back.*)

BRUNNHILDA.

Peace with your clamoring
torrent of words!
You are all my betrayers:
I've come here for my revenge.
(*She calmly advances.*)
You are children
whining to your mother
about the milk you have spilled!
I've heard no words
of fitting lament
for the noblest man that lived.

GUTRUNA.
(*rising from the floor*)

Brunnhilda! Hatred's victim!
You were the bringer of woe
and you aroused the men against him
just when you came into this house.

BRUNNHILDA.

> Poor creature, peace!
> You never were wife of his,
> but only his mistress, no more.
> But I was his lawful wife.
> He pledged me eternal devotion.
> ere he had seen your face!

GUTRUNA.
(in indignant despair)

> Accursed Hagen!
> You urged me give
> the treacherous drink
> that made Siegfried change!
> Ah, sorrow! Sorrow!
> I see it all now!
> *(She turns away in shame from Siegfried, and
> bends fainting over Gunther's body. In this
> position she remains until the end.)*

> Brunnhild was his true love
> the cup compelled him forget!
> *(Hagen stands leaning defiantly on his spear
> and shield, sunk in gloomy meditation.)*

BRUNNHILDA.
(turning to all)

> Let great logs
> be brought to the bank
> and heaped in a mighty pile.
> Let the flames
> leap to the sky
> and consume the noble corpse
> of this first of all men.
> And bring Grane, his horse,
> that we both may follow our hero,
> for I long to share with my body
> the holiest honor due to this man.
> Fulfill Brunnhilda's word!
> *(The young men erect, during the following,
> before the hall, a huge funeral pyre. The*

*women deck it with herbs and flowers. Brunn-
hilda is rapt in contemplation of the body of
Siegfried.)*

He dazzles like the
sun in his strength!
The purest was he,
yet he played false!
Disloyal to Brunnhild,
yet loyal to friendship,
he set up a weapon,
placed it between us,
barring love from his love.
No one was truer,
swearing pledges;
no one was truer
in truth to compacts;
never was man
purer in loving.
Yet in all his pledges,
all of his compacts,
all love and all honor—
none failed as did he!
Know you how that was?

(looking up)

O you, who guard
the honor of pledges!
Look for a while
on my flourishing woe!
Look down on the guilt that is yours!
Hear my sad complaint,
O god most high!
Through Siegfried's highest of deeds,
which you hoped for so much,
doom from your hand
fell on his head,
the curse that must soon strike Wotan.
He—purest
of heroes betrayed me,
that thus a wife might be wise!

Do I know what you want?

All things! All things!
All are known now!
All is clear to me now!
Hark to your ravens!
Hear their rustling?
With tidings long awaited
let me send both of them home.
Henceforth quiet, O god!
(*She signs to the men to bear Siegfried's
body to the funeral pyre, and draws from his
    finger the ring, which she contemplates.*)

The dower comes
back to Brunnhilda.
Accursed round!
Terrible ring!
I now grasp you
and cast you away!
O wise and knowing
water maidens,
you gliding girls of the river,
thank you for sound, frank advice.
What you desire
you now shall have.
From out my ashes
take your possession!
The fire that burns my frame
cleanses the ring of its curse!
You in the Rhine,
wash it away,
and safely preserve
the gleaming gold,
that once was robbed to your bane.
(*She turns to Siegfried's body on the pyre,
    and takes a huge firebrand from a man.*)

Fly home, you ravens!
Whisper to your ruler
the things you heard by the Rhine.

And go by the way of Brunnhild's rock!
The place still blazes.
Send the fire-god
to Valhall,
For the final dusk
has come to all gods!
So—now hurl the brand
at Valhall's glittering pomp.
*(She flings the torch into the pyre, which
quickly kindles brightly. Two ravens fly up
from the rocks by the shore and disappear.
Brunnhilda perceives the horse, led on by
two men.)*

Grane, my horse!
We meet once more!
*(She springs toward him, and unbridles him,
then bends affectionately to him.)*

Do you know, my friend,
just where we are faring?
In radiant fires
there lies your lord,
Siegfried, the lord of my life.
You're joyfully neighing
just to be with him?
Laughter of flames
allures you to follow?
Feel how my bosom
so hotly burns.
Radiant fire
takes hold of my heart.
On to embrace him,
to live in his arms,
thus yoked to him ever
in mightiest love!
Heiajaho! Grane!
Give your lord greeting!
*(She springs to the horse's back and raises
him for a leap.)*

Siegfried! Siegfried! See!

Brunnhild hails you with joy!

*(She urges the horse with one leap into the
burning pyre. The fire blazes high, filling the
entire space before the hall, which it seems
about to devour. The men and women in
terror crowd toward the extreme front. When
all seems wrapped in flames the glow is suddenly extinguished so that only a cloud of
smoke is seen which lies upon the horizon like
a fogbank. At the same time the Rhine up-
swells mightily and pours its waters over the
pyre. The three Rhine-maidens are riding
the waves and appear by the pyre. Hagen,
who has watched Brunnhilda's activities with
increasing anxiety, is alarmed on the appear-
ance of the Rhine daughters. He flings away
his spear, shield and helmet, and madly
plunges into the flood, crying)*

The ring is mine!

*(Voglinda and Vellgunda twine their arms round his neck
and draw him down below. Flosshilda holds up the recovered
ring joyously. Through the cloud bank breaks an increasing red
glow. In its light the Rhine is observed to have returned to its
bed, and the girls are circling and playing with the ring on the
calm water. From the ruins of the half-burnt hall the men and
women perceive with awe the light in the sky, in which now
appears the Hall of Valhalla, where the gods and heroes are
seen sitting together. Bright flames seize on the abode of the
gods.)*

THE END